£9.95

PHILOSOPH
ISSUES I
MORAL EDUCATION
AND
DEVELOPMENT

PHILOSOPHICAL ISSUES IN MORAL EDUCATION AND DEVELOPMENT

Edited by

BEN SPIECKER
Department of Educational Studies
Free University, Amsterdam

and

ROGER STRAUGHAN
School of Education
University of Reading

Open University Press
Milton Keynes · Philadelphia

Open University Press
Open University Educational Enterprises Limited
12 Cofferidge Close
Stony Stratford
Milton Keynes MK11 1BY

and
242 Cherry Street
Philadelphia, PA 19106, USA

First Published 1988

British Library Cataloguing in Publication Data

Philosophical issues in moral education
  and development.
  1. Schools. Moral education. Philosophical
  perspectives
  I. Spiecker, Ben   II. Straughan, Roger, 1941–
  370.11′4

  ISBN 0-335-15851-X
  ISBN 0-335-15850-1 Pbk

Library of Congress Cataloging-in-Publication Data

Philosophical issues in moral education and development/edited by
Ben Spiecker and Roger Straughan.
  Includes bibliographies and index.
  1. Moral education—Congresses.   I. Spiecker, Ben, 1943–
II. Straughan, Roger.   III. Vrije Universiteit te Amsterdam.
LC268.P47 1988   370.11′4—dc19   88-2914
ISBN 0-335-15851-X   ISBN 0-335-15850-1 (pbk.)

Typeset by Gilbert Composing Services
Printed in Great Britain by J.W. Arrowsmith Ltd., Bristol

Contents

Acknowledgements

The material of chapter 4 was derived from the Tanner lecture 'Moderation, Rationality, and Virtue', delivered by Professor Slote at Stanford University on 17 and 18 April 1985, and published in *The Tanner Lectures on Human Values*, Vol. VII (Salt Lake City and Cambridge: The University of Utah Press and Cambridge University Press, 1986). The editors would like to thank Ines Girisch for facilitating this project and for typing the manuscript.

Contributors

DR WOLFGANG BREZINKA is Professor of Education at the University of Konstanz, West Germany.

DR WOUTER VAN HAAFTEN is Professor of Philosophy of Education at the Catholic University of Nijmegen, The Netherlands.

DR MICHAEL SLOTE is Professor of Philosophy at the University of Maryland, College Park, USA.

DR BEN SPIECKER is Professor of Philosophy and History of Education at the Free University of Amsterdam, The Netherlands.

DR JAN STEUTEL is Senior Lecturer in Philosophy of Education at the Free University of Amsterdam, The Netherlands.

DR ROGER STRAUGHAN is Reader in Education at the University of Reading, England.

Introduction

In April 1986, the Free University of Amsterdam organized an international congress on the philosophy of moral education and development. Papers were presented by R.R. Straughan, an Englishman, by M. Slote, an American, by W. Brezinka, a German, and by three Dutch philosophers of education, A.W. van Haaften, B. Spiecker and J.W. Steutel. All these papers have been revised for inclusion in this collection.

As could be expected from such an international company, the contributions are coloured by the varied interests and specific expertise of the authors. Despite this diversity, however, a certain communality can be perceived. In the *subject matter*, as well as in the *method*, there are clear similarities. With regard to the subject matter, in all contributions a certain aspect of the general aim of moral education, the development of the moral person, forms the centre of interest. In each case a certain characteristic of the morally educated person (a mental quality that is supposed to be present or absent) is discussed, and the possible consequences for (the nature of) moral education and development are pointed out. With regard to the method, in general the style of philosophizing is analytic. Certain concepts, especially those that pick out the characteristics of the moral person, are

1

analysed; and problems are approached and elucidated by distinguishing painstakingly their constitutive components. It is within this shared framework that the authors go their own way.

In all contributions due attention is given to the dispositions (propensities, capacities, habits, etc.) of the moral person. The capacity of moral reasoning is one disposition that has in recent years attracted a great deal of attention. Particularly in the cognitive–structuralist paradigm, exemplified by Piaget and Kohlberg, moral education is considered to be a matter of stimulating the development of moral thinking. In his contribution, Van Haaften explores the consequences of this approach in particular for the justification of moral education. If the development of the structure of moral reasoning is seen as passing through qualitatively different stages, how then can parents and educators *justify* their moral practices to their children? And if this possibility is, to a certain extent, ruled out, how can this be compatible with the idea that offering a rational account is an essential component of our concept of morality?

It would be a regrettable misconception to narrow moral education to the promotion of the capacity for moral reasoning. In his article, Straughan explains unequivocally that morality is a complex mixture of judgements and actions. In moral education we must not only pay attention to the ability of the child to reason morally, but also make sure that the child *acts* in accordance with his moral insights. In other words, the child has to acquire not only the capacity to reason in a morally adequate manner, but the *tendency* or *propensity* to act morally as well. And attention to these propensities is given in theories of moral emotions and virtues.

Moral emotions are also part of the equipment of the morally educated person. These emotions are dispositions with a motivating component; the occurrence of moral emotions is accompanied by the tendency to do something. In his essay, Spiecker draws a distinction between two subclasses of moral emotions. The first type, the so-called *rule*-emotions, is connected with the opinion of the actor that a moral rule is applicable to a certain situation. The second type of moral emotions, the so-called *altruistic* emotions, is associated with the actor's understanding of the weal and woe of his fellow man. These two subclasses of emotions are mutually related. From a *developmental* point of view, the presence of altruistic emotions forms a condition for the genesis of rule-emotions; but from a viewpoint of *justification*, the relation is the other way around – the legitimation of the scope and the development of altruistic emotions rests on the rule-emotions. Does this distinction between the two types of moral emotions lead to a better understanding of the controversy between Kohlberg and Gilligan concerning the existence of a male and female domain of morality?

The possession of certain virtues is also accompanied by specific propensities. That applies, among other things, to the trait of character that is analysed by Slote: 'satisficing moderation'. A great many philosophers argue that, in situations in which the interests of one's fellows are not at stake, it is rational and laudable to maximize one's own well-being. In opposition to this model of practical rationality, Slote places a *non*-optimizing form of moderation. The bearer of this virtue is characterized by moderate wants and needs. He is satisfied with 'good enough' and is *not* inclined to strive after a maximum overall satisfaction. Slote argues that this disposition is rational and commendable. Consequently, he pleads for empirical studies of the education and development of this kind of moderation.

In Brezinka's essay, another quality of the moral person takes a central place: competence (in German: *Tüchtigkeit*). Competence is considered by Brezinka to be, like the Greek aretè, a relatively permanent ability enabling an individual to meet specific demands to their full extent. To strive after this ideal of personality, as an aim of education, excludes practising certain alternative conceptions of moral education, for example all forms of *nativism* and *evolutionism*. The development of competence is no process of natural maturation, but is in the first place dependent on personal effort and the initiation into culture. Furthermore, the ideal of competence is not consonant with forms of *intellectualism*, which Brezinka senses in certain texts of Kohlberg. In intellectualism the importance of the development of reasoning by cognitive stimulation is stressed; but in order to acquire competence the development of emotions and tendencies is especially required. And for that purpose, habituation seems to be the most appropriate method.

Yet the combination of the capacity for moral reasoning (a developed judgemental structure) and the presence of the adequate propensities (moral emotions and certain virtues) does not guarantee the execution of the proper moral action. The occurrence of (counter-)inclinations can prevent the execution of the right actions. That is, for instance, the case with a person who is morally weak, or who is not capable of controlling himself.

According to Straughan, in the case of moral weakness there is an inconsistency between what a person thinks he ought to do and what he in fact does. To elucidate this discrepancy Straughan introduces the distinction between *justificatory* and *motivating* reasons. The agent *explicitly* acknowledges that there are proper moral reasons for the realization of a certain action (justificatory reasons). At the same time, however, the agent *in fact* gives more weight to his inclination to do something else (motivating reasons). In other words, the sincere acknowledgement of the validity of moral reasons is not a sufficient condition for the execution of the action. In cases of moral weakness a person will, under the influence of certain inclinations, award greater priority to non-moral considerations.

The fact that (counter-)inclinations can result in improper conduct, can also be a consequence of a certain lack of self-control. According to Steutel, the acquisition of self-control is primarily to be seen as the learning of subtle and varied *techniques of self-intervention*. Partly due to the efforts of the older generation, the child learns to control his (counter-)inclinations by intervening in his wants and aversions in the right way and at the right time. If the virtue of self-control indeed is the complex ability of effective self-intervention, we can, according to Steutel, draw two conclusions. First, the so-called motivation theory of virtues and vices, which states that virtues, as opposed to abilities, enclose certain wants or aversions, does not apply to the virtue of self-control. Secondly, if a child shows a lack of self-control (a complaint often raised by teachers) this can be attributed to insufficient *training* in the techniques of self-intervention.

Ultimately moral education is aimed at the child learning to act in a morally right manner. To attain this ultimate aim, it certainly is necessary to stimulate the development of moral reasoning. But the road from moral reasoning to moral action is often long and laborious. Not only do we have to be motivated to translate our moral judgements into actions, which requires that we have acquired moral emotions and virtues; in addition we have to be free from moral weakness and able to exert self-control. In this collection of articles the authors aim for a better understanding of certain aspects of this road from moral reasoning to moral action.

B.S.
J.S.
R.S.

Judgement and action in moral education

ROGER STRAUGHAN

The relationship between judgement and action in both moral and non-moral contexts raises questions which have exercised philosophers for centuries. Some of these questions have interesting implications for the areas of moral education and moral development, which philosophers have recently started to explore in company with psychologists, sociologists and educationalists. The purpose of this chapter is to examine some of these implications, first by drawing attention to some general, fundamental features of moral education and moral development, and secondly by focussing upon one specific problem within moral education.

The first task is to underline a few obvious but important points about why the philosophical issue of 'judgement and action' must lie at the very heart of moral education and development – indeed at the heart of morality itself. The nature of morality consists of a complex mixture and interaction of judgements and actions, of beliefs and behaviour. I am behaving morally when I act in accordance with certain judgements, reasons and intentions which lead me to believe that I *ought* to act in that way. It follows that we cannot look merely at a person's outward behaviour to determine whether or not he is acting morally. The same piece of outward behaviour (handing over some money, for example) can be interpreted in many different ways because of the many different reasons and intentions which may lie behind it. We cannot begin to judge whether the action of handing over some money on a particular occasion could be called 'moral', 'non-moral' or 'immoral', without knowing something of the agent's reasons and intentions – though of course philosophers are far from being agreed about precisely what *kind* of reasons and intentions are required for moral action.

Most philosophers and non-philosophers, however, probably would agree that, although having certain reasons and intentions of some kind is a *necessary* part of being a moral agent, this cannot be *sufficient* to constitute moral agency, for those intentions and motives must also lead one actually to perform the appropriate action. Morality is, by definition, a practical business, in that it is basically concerned with what ought to be done, and what it is right to do. Working out answers to moral problems and dilemmas in a purely theoretical way, as one solves a crossword clue, is not alone enough to qualify as 'being moral' if there is no consequent attempt made to act in accordance with one's conclusions.

Therefore, no adequate account of morality can be given *just* in terms of making particular kinds of judgement, or *just* in terms of performing particular kinds of action. Morality must refer to how a person both thinks and behaves. And if that is true of morality itself, it must also be true of moral education and moral development. No account of moral education or development, then, can be adequate if it concentrates exclusively either upon children's judgements and reasoning or upon their actions and behaviour.

Now this is where these apparently obvious points about the nature of morality start to assume some real practical importance, because many approaches to moral education and development fall into the trap of ignoring this complex balance between judgement and action and of overemphasizing one at the expense of the other.

There is, for example, one influential psychological tradition which has tried to study moral development predominantly in terms of children's moral *judgements*. Within this tradition, which goes back at least to Piaget's pioneering work in the 1930s, the level of thinking shown in a moral conflict situation, the cognitive complexity of the child's moral judgement and the type of reason given to justify a decision have been among the major factors thought most relevant in assessing moral development. Developmental psychologists, then, have tended to see moral development as concerned primarily with the form or structure of children's moral thinking, and characterized not so much by what the child actually does as by the reasons why he thinks he ought or ought not to do it. The classic expression of this view is to be found in the Foreword to Piaget's (1932) highly influential book, 'The Moral Judgment of the Child', where he states:

> Readers will find in this book no direct analysis of child morality as it is practised in home and school life or in children's societies. It is the moral judgment that we propose to investigate, not moral behaviour or sentiments.

Lawrence Kohlberg and his associates are to some extent the modern representatives of this tradition – though I am not suggesting that either Piaget or Kohlberg totally ignore moral action and behaviour. Both have some interesting things to say on that subject, but nevertheless the main thrust of their work and indeed their whole methodology is directed towards an investigation of moral judgement and reasoning rather than moral actions and behaviour.

Now, this 'judgemental' approach to moral development has had an undoubted effect upon modern conceptions of moral education. Traditional notions of moral training or instruction, aimed at inculcating in children a particular code of moral conduct (e.g. telling the truth, respecting one's elders, playing one's hardest for the school), have largely been replaced by an emphasis upon furthering children's understanding of moral issues by teaching 'moral skills' and methods of moral reasoning – though moral education programmes in the British Isles have not gone quite so far as the Canadian Mackay Report on Moral Development, for example, which

8

leaned heavily on Kohlberg's work for its theoretical backing and stated baldly: 'We equate character development with the development of the ability to reason morally' (Committee on Religious Education in the Public Schools of Ontario, 1969).

In contrast to these 'judgemental' approaches, there are opposing traditions, which seem to overemphasize behaviour at the expense of judgement – for example, the psychological, behaviourist tradition and its modern manifestation, behaviour modification. So we find B.F. Skinner, for example, maintaining that accounts of morality should avoid all reference to 'mentalistic phenomena' like beliefs and intentions, and to concepts of choice, responsibility and justice; a person acts morally not because he knows or feels that his behaviour is right, but because of the 'contingencies' which have 'shaped his behaviour' (Skinner, 1974: 193).

Again, we can see this 'behavioural' approach to morality reflected in certain conceptions of moral education, or perhaps in this case moral training. The whole aim of the educational exercise on this view is that children should be taught or made to 'behave properly'. Levels of judgement and quality of reasoning are all very well, but it is what the child does that ultimately counts. New courses may be introduced in schools, aimed at getting children to discuss moral questions, but it is standards of behaviour (in and out of school) which signify the success or failure of moral teaching.

To summarize, then, this first very general and very obvious point, if we focus excessively or exclusively upon *either* judgement *or* action in our approach to moral education and moral development, we are distorting the very nature of morality, which consists of a complex interaction *between* judgement and action. Both judgemental and behavioural criteria must be satisfied before we can say that moral education has succeeded or that moral development has taken place.

This first point leads directly to the second. This concerns a specific, practical problem, which moral education often fails to tackle – the problem of moral weakness, of which we should

9

all have plenty of practical experience in our daily lives – unless we are saints!

What has been said so far about judgement and action strongly implies the possibility of moral weakness. For example, the claim has been made that even if a child has learned skills which satisfy certain judgemental criteria for moral reasoning, this cannot be sufficient to demonstrate that he has been successfully morally educated, for he may fail to act upon the judgement which he has formed. There is, on the face of it, no reason to deny that a child (or adult) may at times judge that he ought to do X, perhaps revealing considerable moral maturity in arriving at this judgement, yet then deliberately fail to do X. Such a person could hardly claim to have acted morally or to have had an effective moral education.

The educational problem of moral weakness, then, is concerned with how to teach or encourage children to act upon their moral judgements, an issue on which I have written at some length elsewhere (Straughan, 1982) and which I shall try to summarize as follows.

What exactly is happening when we fail to act upon our moral judgements, when we are guilty of moral weakness? Many different types of explanation are possible, and each explanation points to a particular kind of method for the moral *educator* to employ in trying to tackle the problem of moral weakness. There are, for example, a number of *causal* explanations, which suggest that we are at times overcome by overpowering emotions, desires or other irrational factors; we are simply not strong enough to withstand these pressures because either our will or our conscience is too weak. So moral education, according to this account, will aim to help children to control or repress their emotions, to build up a strong character and conscience, and to increase their will-power.

These causal, mechanistic explanations are not in my view convincing (Straughan, 1982: Ch. 4). There is no reason to suppose that any distinct mental organ, called the 'will' or 'conscience', exists and can be identified, and we should not therefore assume the existence of such entities merely to explain why we at times fail to do what we believe we ought to do; one cannot explain that sort of phenomenon simply by inventing labels like 'weak will' to describe it (see, e.g. Hirst, 1974: 70–71).

What is happening in so-called cases of 'moral weakness' is not a battle between our 'will' (whatever that might be) and our emotions, but rather a conflict or incompatibility between two different kinds of reason for action.

The notion of a 'reason for action' is in fact highly ambiguous, which can and does lead to a lot of confusion. Reasons can justify and they can motivate. These two functions are logically separate, though they may often combine in practice. If I believe that I ought to do X, I am acknowledging that there are good justificatory reasons for my doing X, which will be derivable from some more generalized principle. I may, for instance, believe that I ought to visit my aunt in hospital, because hospital patients generally like to be visited and cheered up, it may help my aunt to recover more quickly, and I would want to be visited if I were in her situation. So I am signifying my agreement with the principle that visiting relatives in hospital is in general a good thing, and am thereby acknowledging that there are good justificatory reasons for visiting my aunt; but I am not necessarily signifying any personal desire or inclination to visit her. Perhaps I do not have the time or the energy, perhaps I dislike my aunt intensely, or perhaps I dislike the atmosphere of hospitals even more intensely. I may, then, have no reason at all which motivates me to visit my aunt, as I would have if I were fond of her or if she were going to leave me all her money.

A crucial distinction, therefore, is being suggested between reasons which justify and reasons which motivate. This distinction offers us a general explanation for the phenomenon of moral weakness: a person may fail to do what he thinks he ought to do because he does not want to do what he thinks he ought to do (or wants to do something else more).

It might, however, be objected at this point that my proposed distinction (upon which the argument of this chapter ultimately depends) is in fact false, or at least too stark. Do not justificatory reasons always carry with them some motivational overtones? May not motivational reasons also provide a justification? Am I not ignoring the possibility of a person (a) being most strongly motivated by those considerations which he feels to be justificatory, or (b) maintaining that whatever he most wants is justified simply because he most wants it?

My reply to such objections would be first that of course we sometimes (perhaps often, and in some saintly cases even always) want to do what we think we ought to do because we believe there are good justificatory reasons for so acting. Inclination and obligation may often coincide in this way, but when they do it is still *two* logically separate kinds of consideration which are on these occasions overlapping. The possibility always remains of a conflict between justificatory and motivational reasons, and it is this conflict which in practice produces instances of moral weakness and indeed provides the whole business of morality with its unique and distinctive tensions. It is always possible and meaningful to ask the question, 'Why should I do what I morally ought to do?' (Frankena, 1958: 47). Secondly, it follows from this that the mere fact of wanting to do something cannot morally justify that action. Moral justifications reach beyond particular personal wants to general principles which by definition are of wider application than individual desires. If everything I want is thereby morally justified, moral justification loses all meaning and becomes a vacuous concept. The distinction between justificatory and motivational reasons must therefore be preserved, though in practice the relationship between the two will often be complex; it is, for example, quite possible to believe *that* X ought to be done and to *want* X to be done, but not to want *to do* X oneself (Straughan, 1982: 50–57).

Can a more detailed picture be painted of this possible conflict between justificatory and motivational reasons? The morally weak person sincerely believes that there are good justificatory reasons why he ought to do X, yet there are also operative motivational reasons for not doing X. These latter reasons will derive from his wants, which lead him to see something else as more desirable than X in some way. What he is doing, then, in effect is to acknowledge explicitly the validity of the justificatory reasons which underlie his ought-judgement, without making explicit the motivational reasons which are in fact weighing more heavily with him at the time of his decision or action. Moral weakness, therefore, appears to involve a particular kind of self-deception or intellectual dishonesty, in so far as the agent, in forming his ought-judgement, fails to spell out to himself (or to others) the motivational factors which are really influencing his course of action. Thus, my belief that I ought to visit my aunt in hospital is only a part of my overall appraisal of the situation. The reasons which justify my visiting her are in practice outweighed by motivational factors such as my fear of hospitals; yet I make explicit only my ought-judgement and my justificatory reasons (which are morally respectable), and avoid reference to my inclinations and my motivational reasons (which are morally disreputable). In this way my apparently puzzling behaviour in not visiting my aunt as I believe I ought comes to be attributed to my 'weakness', whereas the real explanation is that I want to avoid hospitals more than I want to visit my aunt (cf. Straughan, 1982: 126–33).

At the heart of so-called 'moral weakness', then, is a refusal to admit and spell out what one really wants most, when expressing one's appraisal of a moral conflict situation. This happens because to make explicit one's overall appraisal would be to admit the greater priority one is assigning to non-moral than to moral considerations. By this means one can misleadingly attribute one's subsequent 'lapse' to over-whelming emotion or a weak will or a weak conscience, all of which appear to offer a partial excuse on the grounds that one did not really choose to behave as one did.

This interpretation of moral weakness explores only one dimension of the problem, but this is not the place for a more detailed analysis (cf. Straughan, 1982: Ch. 6). Even this single dimension, however, yields some interesting implications for moral education, to which we can now finally turn.

It could be objected at this point that the educational implications of my interpretation are in fact very limited. Even if, the argument might go, we can teach children to make more honest and open appraisals of their wants and motives, this is not necessarily going to overcome the problem of moral weakness and make it more likely that a child will act upon his moral judgements. He will simply have a fuller understanding and a more open acceptance of his reasons for acting as he does, so becoming a more self-aware egotist than he was before.

My reply to that objection would be that it is surely necessary as a first step to be aware of what one most wants before one can start to re-examine or consciously modify those wants. So any teaching methods which start by encouraging children to acknowledge and explore what their present wants and motives are may also be influential in leading them to make more considered appraisals of those wants and motives and consequently perhaps to modify them. If my interpretation of moral weakness is valid, it follows that it can only be combated by modifying one's wants in some way and by making one's motivational reasons for action coincide with the justificatory ones.

What teaching methods might help to produce this kind of self-knowledge? Direct instruction seems unlikely to achieve very much, though there could be some value in introducing older children to some psychological and sociological theories of motivation. Group discussion also has certain built-in drawbacks, as it will inevitably take place within the context of group norms and expectations, which will establish what are acceptable, respectable priorities and values within the group; this could inhibit the individual child from acknowledging his own priorities, even to himself.

If self-deception and intellectual dishonesty are to be avoided, therefore, the moral educator will need to foster an atmosphere that is as free as possible from conventional constraints, where children do not feel vulnerable to moral censure. Mutual consideration and sympathetic understanding within the group will be prerequisites here. If a non-censorious ethos of this kind can be created, there should be more chance of a child acknowledging, examining and appraising his motivational reasons for action (e.g. why he prefers playing football with his friends to looking after his little sister), and consequently less danger of him merely saying what he thinks he is expected to say (e.g. 'I ought to look after my little sister more often'). Some of the recent approaches to personal, social and moral education, such as values clarification and active tutorial work, might be used for this purpose (cf. Raths, Harmin and Simon, 1978; Button, 1982).

The more traditional methods of moral exhortation and preaching seem likely to prove counter-productive if used to combat moral weakness, for they are designed to establish precisely the kind of censorious atmosphere in which the notion of moral weakness has its natural home. Such an atmosphere will encourage the explicit expression of justificatory reasons and will discourage the admission of motivational ones if they appear to be morally disreputable.

If moral education, then, is to take proper account of the problem of moral weakness, it must guard against the child setting his moral sights too high or having them set for him too high, initially at least. Unrealistic moral demands, whether self-imposed or externally imposed, can result only in failure, discouragement, and either cynicism or a guilt-ridden retreat to self-deception and the misleading excuse of a 'weak will'. This conclusion is perhaps best summed up in a passage by John Benson (1968: 172), which should give food for thought to moral educators as well as to moral philosophers.

> I should welcome the recognition that the suppression of desires is sometimes just not worth the sweat and one would do better to adopt a principle which is easier to live with. Writers on ethics still tend to speak as though the task of the will is to beat the passions into submission in the interests of morality. There is also the task of exploring one's powers in order to discover what principles one can realistically commit oneself to. Weakness of will is sometimes what, in our zeal for self-castigation, we call the inevitable result of moral hubris.

This notion of 'exploring one's powers in order to discover what principles one can realistically commit oneself to' could be said to offer a controversial definition of what moral education and development fundamentally consist of. Such a definition would of course need a lengthy investigation and defence if it were to be sustained; one obvious objection, for example, would concern the *level* of principles required to count as 'moral'. Moral principles presumably cannot be *too* easy to live with if the distinction between justificatory and motivational considerations is to be upheld. Nevertheless, Benson's account, which suggests some interesting links with some recent theological work on self-awareness and self-acceptance (cf. Williams, 1972, 1965), goes some way towards bridging the inevitable gap between judgement and action, which must, however, always remain a necessary component of morality itself and thereby a central concern of moral education.

References

Benson, J. (1968). Oughts and Wants. *Proceedings of the Aristotelian Society*, **XLII**.

Button, L. (1982). *Group Tutoring for the Form Teacher*. London.

Committee on Religious Education in the Public Schools of Ontario (1969). *Religious Information and Moral Development*. Toronto.

Frankena, W.K. (1958). Obligation and Motivation. *In* A.I. Melden (ed.), *Essays in Moral Philosophy*. Seattle and London.

Hirst, P.H. (1974). *Moral Education in a Secular Society*. London.

Piaget, J. (1932). *The Moral Judgment of the Child*. London.

Raths, L., Harmin, M. and Simon, S. (1978). *Values and Teaching*. Columbus.

Skinner, B.F. (1974). *About Behaviourism*. London.

Straughan, R. (1982). *I Ought to, But...: A Philosophical Approach to the Problem of Weakness of Will in Education*. Windsor.

Williams, H. (1965). *The Time Wilderness*. London.

Williams, H. (1972). *True Resurrection*. London.

Can moral education be justified in moral education?

WOUTER VAN HAAFTEN

The justification of education, including moral education, seems to have always been conceived of as something between adults. However, should we not first of all justify moral education to the child who is to be educated? But can we? Can a justification of moral education be provided to children who (by definition) are at a lower level of moral development?

A considerable part of moral education takes place in the form of conversations about what should be done (or should have been done) in particular situations and why. It is part of our very concept of morality that we ought to be able to adduce adequate grounds for what we say and do, and it certainly is one of the aspects of what we want to develop in moral education. Through discussions and deliberations we hope to further the child's moral development. During this process, not only the child but also the moral educator will have to put forward his reasons for what he says and does. First of all, because he ought to set the example; but, secondly, and more importantly, this is also required by the essentially mutual character of what it is to give reasons. The serious giving of reasons has a moral aspect of itself. It implies that all parties concerned will give their reasons, that they put forward their best possible reasons, and that they will accept the

17

consequences if better reasons are adduced. Moreover, all parties should in principle be willing to argue about any relevant subject-matter, be it one's own or other persons' thoughts or judgements, feelings and intentions or actions – in short, anything we think or do. But this certainly includes moral education itself as provided by the educator. Therefore, much of moral education takes place in, and in the form of, the mutual giving of reasons, and in this regard the justification of moral education should in principle form part of the moral education to be justified.

The question, however, is whether this is possible. One may concede many of the criticisms that have been levelled against cognitive structuralistic theories of moral development (e.g. Piaget, 1932; Kohlberg, 1976; Kohlberg *et al.*, 1983; cf. e.g. Modgil and Modgil, 1986; Locke, 1986) without rejecting one important insight which is at their heart, viz., the idea of development through qualitatively different forms or stages of moral reasoning. If we only accept this much, however, we will have to face the question as to how far the *justification* of moral education can be possible to the child who is at a different developmental stage. How can the furtherance of a development towards increasingly better ways of dealing with moral problems be justified to those who *ex hypothesi* cannot yet fully understand and appreciate these allegedly better forms of moral judgement, and who therefore cannot see why they should have to move into that direction?

On the one hand, moral education seems to require such a possibility because justification itself is part of our very notion of morality; whereas, on the other hand, if we conceive moral development as the gaining of really new ways of handling moral situations, and moral education as to be contributing to this, the requisite justification cannot be given. In order to map out this problem, I would like to do two things. First I will elaborate and perhaps slightly sharpen some relevant points in the cognitive structuralistic notion of moral development. Secondly, I will face up to the implications for the possibility of justification in moral education.

In Section 1, I distinguish two levels at which we might claim moral development and therefore might have to justify our claim, namely within stages and from stage to stage. In Section 2, some consequences of conceiving stages as qualitatively different ways of conceptualizing (moral) reality are drawn, especially with regard to the question of how far the justification of moral judgements is dependent on the stage one is at. In Section 3, I try to elucidate the relation between genesis and justification, in particular in the case of 'internal' justification which typically is made possible by, and at the same time makes an appeal to, the development in question. After these explorations into the cognitive structuralistic perspective on moral development, I will conclude in Section 4 that, although extreme forms of relativism are not at issue, justifications in moral education – including justifications of moral education – can indeed only be given in terms of the stage the child is at. In Section 5, I try to mitigate this conclusion and to explore some ways in which justification nevertheless can play an important role in moral education.

1 Two levels of justification

Moral education presupposes a certain conception of morality and of the way moral problems should be handled. In the cognitive structuralistic paradigm several qualitatively different stages are distinguished in moral development, or rather, in the way moral dilemmas are being resolved. These stages are held to be universal and to follow an invariant sequence of development, in which each later stage is considered better, or more adequate, than preceding ones. Part of moral education is therefore directed towards stimulating the child to acquire higher stage forms of moral reasoning. The justification of this kind of moral education should therefore consist in an argument showing that the pattern of moral reasoning which is typical for the higher stage, is the morally more adequate way of dealing with moral problems. I propose to pursue these cognitive structuralistic intuitions and to see where they lead us. One may be fully aware – as is Kohlberg himself – of the

19

onesidedness of so much emphasis on the moral reasoning aspect. But it surely is *one* aspect of morality, and a vital one for that matter. For the moment we may restrict ourselves to this aspect.

Let us first make a clear distinction between two levels of evaluating and justifying moral development claims. I do not mean developmental stages here, but rather logically different levels at which the term 'moral development' might be appropriate, and at which a person might want to defend developmental claims. They roughly correspond to Kohlberg's distinction between form and content, but this distinction merits some elaboration.

If we put on a zero level the ordinary things people (including ourselves) think and do, then the *first* level that I would like to distinguish is the level of *judgements about such concrete actions and thoughts*. At this level we do three things.[1] First, we *interpret* these actions and thoughts in a certain way;[2] secondly, we may *evaluate* them; and thirdly, we may give our *reasons*, both for the interpretation and for the evaluation. For instance, I see something happen and I infer: 'This must be Heinz stealing drugs from the drugstore' (interpretation), and I say something like 'People should not steal drugs' (evaluation), for which I may put forward my reasons (justification). I might thereupon have a discussion with some friends, arguing whether Heinz ought or ought not to steal those drugs. (You will know the story: the drugs are for his wife, who is dying, and for whom Heinz has desperately but vainly been trying to get the drugs in a legal way.) All of this takes place at the first level of judgements concerning concrete actions and thoughts.

As said before, Kohlberg, in his theory of moral development, distinguishes several qualitatively *different ways of moral reasoning* about such questions, which he considers to be representative of different stages in moral development. Each stage has its own specific manner of resolving moral dilemmas concerning concrete thoughts (or statements) and actions. That is to say, we may interpret a certain pattern of arguing as typical of one moral stage, and another kind of argument as typical of another stage. In doing so, however, we are judging at what I would like to call the *second level*. This is the level, not of what we say concerning concrete statements and actions, but of *judgements concerning ways of reasoning about such concrete events.* At this level again there is *interpretation* (what kind of moral reasoning is this?), *evaluation* (is it an adequate way of dealing with moral problems?), and *justification* (argument about either interpretation and/or evaluation).

Therefore, there are two levels of moral reasoning. At the first level we talk *about* concrete actions and thoughts. At the second level we talk *about* the way we talk about concrete actions and thoughts. We may bring this into a schema as follows (to be read from below upwards):

Evaluations and justifications, as you can see, come in at both levels. For instance, at the first level: 'What Peter really does is...', 'What Peter does is right because...', or 'What Peter does is better than what John did in the same situation.'

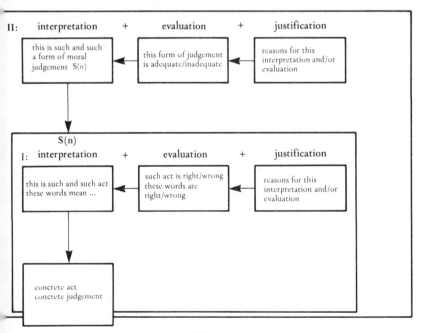

And notice that we can also point to a kind of *development* here: 'What Peter does now is much better than what he used to do in similar situations.' At the second level we justify our judgements about these sorts of judgements about concrete actions or statements. For instance: 'This is really the way moral dilemmas should be dealt with, because ...', or 'Peter's way of dealing with moral dilemmas is better (morally more adequate) than John's.' And here again we can point to a kind of development: 'Peter's way of dealing with such and such moral dilemmas now is totally different from and much better than the way he used to handle them some years ago.'

So there can be development at both levels. Moral development as it is conceived in cognitive structuralist theories, however, is development of only the *second* sort. That is to say, at level II a distinction is made between several *forms* of interpretation, evaluation and especially justification occurring at level I (forms of approaching concrete moral problems), and these forms are regarded as characteristic of sequential stages S(1), S(2), S(3), ...[3] We may call such a level II claim a *descriptive developmental claim*, because of its more or less explicit definition or demarcation of the respective developmental stages. To this descriptive claim one may add an evaluation, for instance one may say that stages 1 to 3 should be considered increasingly better or morally more adequate forms of moral reasoning (interpretation, evaluation, justification) at level I. We may call this additional claim the *evaluative developmental claim*.[4] Our schema can now be amplified (see Schema II).[5]

In short, we might speak *at level I* of moral development, as an improvement in how concrete moral situations are judged and handled. In this case, our criteria in judging development may be derived from (or rather, are representative of) one specific Kohlbergian stage. Or, we might speak *at level II* of moral development, in the sense of a passing through several such Kohlbergian stages. Kohlbergian development is of the latter sort. In that case, the criterion is problematic. Before we come back to this point, some more comments are needed on the cognitive structuralistic notion of developmental stages.

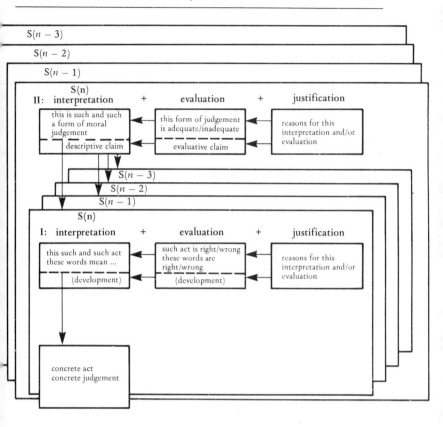

2 Conceptualizational development

Especially in their more theoretical speculations, cognitive structuralists tend to characterize stages as qualitatively different *structures d'ensemble* (e.g. Piaget, 1960; Piaget and Inhelder, 1969) or 'structured wholes' (e.g. Kohlberg, 1969, 1981). In spite of much criticism (e.g. Bickhard, 1978; Brainerd, 1978; Longeot, 1978; Vuyk, 1981) Kohlberg seems to adhere to this notion of stages. He sees them as 'total ways of thinking', 'systems of internal relations', 'rules for the processing of information' (Kohlberg, 1981:57). A stage, according to Kohlberg '... represents an underlying thought-organization' and, he continues: 'The implication is that various aspects of

23

stage structures should appear as a consistent cluster of responses in development' (Kohlberg, 1984: 238).

The idea of stages as 'conceptual frameworks' can be traced back to the historical roots of the paradigm. Kant (1781) reconciled the opposition between empiricism and rationalism by interpreting knowledge as a result of mediation of experience through mental structures. Piaget held to this basic notion but, in addition, he wanted to account for the development of these mediating mental structures. In Kohlberg's writings they reappear as stage-specific forms of 'thought-organization' underlying moral judgement. So Kant's transcendental conditions for the possibility of human knowledge are translated into the various *forms* of judgement characteristic of the qualitatively different stages in moral development.

According to this line of thought moral developmental stages can thus best be seen as different ways of conceptualizing part of reality, viz., the moral domain. In moral development there are then not only changes in the way concrete moral dilemmas (like Kohlberg's Heinz-dilemma) are resolved. Nor is it only a change in the general approach to moral questions. There is an attendant change in our conception of morality itself. In a new stage we not only conceive and resolve moral dilemmas in a new manner, but we also – albeit implicitly most of the time – come to new answers to the question of *what morality is*, what actually moral problems are, what is the specific character of moral judgement altogether, including new emotional connotations and evaluations, for instance in the way interpersonal relations are experienced.[6] For this reason I will use the term 'conceptualizational development'.

The above might be put in another way. If we take seriously the basic intuition that there are qualitatively different stages in moral development – at least as they are distinguished in our thinking or theory about moral development at level II – then we can say that each distinct stage is characterized by its own *specific foundations of morality* (cf. Boyd, 1986). It is precisely because of these different foundations of morality that in each stage we deal with moral problems in an *essentially* different way. It is also precisely on account of these different foundations that we justify our moral judgements and evaluations differently.

And there is something to be added to this. A new stage may now bring along not only new forms of moral reasoning and new arguments in justifying moral decisions, not only a new concept of morality, but also a new perspective on what it is to justify moral decisions – in other words, a new concept of *justification*. For instance, if in an early stage of moral development a child says he does something in order to avoid punishment, whereas later on there is some sort of autonomous principled thinking and argument, it is clear that in those two stages there is not only a qualitatively different sort of moral reasoning, but also an essentially different conception of *what it is to give reasons* for what you are thinking and doing. That we should carefully weigh all relevant considerations without any sort of prejudice, for instance, is itself an insight of only a much later stage in moral development.

If the foregoing is correct, then in a double sense we may say that our justification of moral judgements and actions is dependent on our own moral development, dependent on the stage we are at. A crucial further question in this connection then is what we are to understand by a stage, and particularly by being 'at' a stage. As is well known, cognitive structuralistic theories are not always very clear about this central concept. A few remarks are due.

First, adapting from Habermas (1981; cf. Van Haaften *et al.*, 1986), we may distinguish between the 'logic' part of a developmental theory, in which the various stages of a certain kind (dimension) of development are defined, demarcated, and their relations described, and the 'dynamic' part, in which actual developmental processes and their conditions are studied. Descriptions and explanations of concrete developmental processes always presuppose a developmental logic, only on the basis of which can there be such a thing as, for example, progress. The stages we discussed above are typically stages as they are reconstructed in the *logic* part.

Secondly, it is now clear that although the stages as defined in the logic are qualitatively and fundamentally different wholes, *factual* development through those stages may be smooth and need not at all for that reason be thought of as proceeding via crisis-like transitions. The *distinction* of essentially different forms of moral reasoning does not say anything directly about the actual developmental process. Thus, there need not be any problem if we should have to conclude that '...children seem psychologically as well as biologically almost always in transition, almost never in a steady state' (Flavell, 1982 : 13). And Kohlberg need not make his stage concept vulnerable to criticism of low empirical confirmation by claiming that there should always be 'a consistent cluster of responses in development' (see above). In this way, the distinction between logic and dynamic can contribute much to meet current objections against stage theories and so to maintain the notion of qualitative development.

Thirdly, we should also distinguish between the description of developmental processes, the explanation of such processes, and the justification of developmental claims such as may be implied by the descriptions and explanations. Stages, as defined in the logic, will perhaps rarely be *descriptively* adequate if this were to mean that they should completely match an observable part of the developmental process. In *explanation*, however, they are indispensable theoretical anchorage-points, because they signpost the essential characteristics in terms of which the development to be explained is defined. Likewise stages, as reconstructed, are presupposed in any *justification* of developmental claims. The justification of moral education, which is based on the justification of an evaluative developmental claim, will always refer to the moral superiority of a *qualitatively different* higher stage to be attained. The comparison between the stages, which in this case necessarily underlies the argument, is in effect – more or less neatly – a comparison of (the) essential characteristics as they are specified in the logic part of the developmental theory.

For the justification of developmental claims, therefore, the qualitative *differences* between the stages are decisive. But what precisely do we mean by saying that stages are 'qualitatively different' – as is one of the fundamental tenets of cognitive structuralistic theories? I think besides specific conditions, the following *two general requirements* are necessary for any theory of conceptualizational development.[7]

On the one hand, a person who (at least with respect to a certain subject matter) reasons according to a stage (n), must, if stages are to be qualitatively different, in principle regard the conceptualizations that are characteristic of the foregoing stage $(n-1)$ as inadequate, or at least as no longer fully adequate.[8] Otherwise he might just as well prefer stage $(n-1)$. In other words, *a typical stage (n minus) argument can no more (or no more fully) be accepted as a valid argument in stage (n)*. In passing you may notice that there is an important presupposition to be made here, namely, that a person who is at stage (n) must have sufficient access to his own former qualitatively different conceptual stages, or at least he must have a sufficient idea of what was characteristic of them, in order to be able to (either consciously or unconsciously) compare them to his actual stage.[9]

On the other hand, a person who typically reasons according to stage (n) should not immediately and by the same token be able to understand *and* appreciate stage$(n+1)$ *to such a degree* that he in fact makes the transition to that stage$(n+1)$. Otherwise he would *ipso facto* be at stage$(n+1)$, and there would be no use for the distinction between stages(n) and $(n+1)$ as two qualitatively different stages. In other words, *a typical stage(n plus) argument cannot yet (or not yet immediately) be accepted as a valid argument in stage(n)*. Incidentally, by this we need not imply that someone at stage(n) should *in fact* always reason and act according to that stage. The point is that we can remind him of the proper way of reasoning according to stage(n) – which would not be possible for him with regard to stage$(n+1)$.

Such must be the difference between stages in the reconstruction of moral development if moral reasoning is part of morality and if stages are to be qualitatively different.[10] This means that confusion results if we say, as is usually done, that the stage a person is 'at' is the stage according to which he reacts to moral dilemmas *most of the time*. A person seldom judges according to just one stage, and in practice he does not always judge along lines which, upon reflection, he would consider most adequate. I think, therefore, that a person should be considered to have reached (and to be *at*) stage(n) *if and as soon as he understands its typical form of moral reasoning and in principle can and, on reflection, does accept that form of moral reasoning as more adequate than that of stage($n-1$)* – in other words, if and as soon as he understands and accepts reasons (at level II) to appreciate ways of dealing with moral problems (at level I) that are characteristic of stage(n) as morally better than those that were characteristic of stage ($n-1$).[11] The stage according to which he reacts most of the time *may* be stage(n), but more often that will be a lower stage (cf. Rest, 1973, 1976).

3 Internal justification of developmental claims

Let me sketch one further implication of interpreting moral development as a form of conceptualizational development. Developmental claims – either descriptive ('such and such stages 1 to 3 can be distinguished') or also evaluative ('stages 1 to 3 show increasingly adequate forms of moral reasoning') – are not necessarily made from an external (*observer*) perspective – for instance, within the framework of an elaborate theory of moral development. Developmental claims may be made by the developing person himself (say, from the *actor* perspective) as well. In that case, this will often be done in a rather rough and implicit way. Each time someone rejects a certain kind of moral reasoning in favour of newly acquired insights, he actually thereby implies some sort of developmental claim. An explicit claim, however, requires that stages be sufficiently clearly distinguished, and evaluated in comparison. In this respect, there is with regard to conceptualizational development no structural difference between actor perspective and observer perspective. Both to a certain degree reconstruct a developmental logic.[12]

In the justification of a developmental claim [13] we give our best possible reasons why we consider changes that have taken place to be a development – in the descriptive sense or (mostly) also in the evaluative sense. The interesting point about the justification of conceptualizational development is that it may be, and usually[14] will be, determined by the development to be justified. In that case we may call it an *internal justification* of a developmental claim. I do not mean by this that the actor should accomplish his development completely by himself. How developments are effected is not my question here. Nor do I mean that the actor should invent his reasons all by himself: someone else may mention them in a discussion, whereupon he may accept them. If developmental stages are really qualitatively different, we can even wonder whether a person could ever himself 'invent' the reasons that are typical for higher stages than he is in – and this only underlines once more the importance of moral *education*. But this is not what I mean by 'internal justification'. Conceptualizational developments, in contradistinction to other sorts of development, allow for internal justification in the sense that *the justification is made possible by, and at the same time makes an appeal to, the development in question.*

Clearly, the internal justification of, for example, an evaluative moral developmental claim can only be given in retrospect. In principle such a justification then consists of the following steps. First, it is pointed out that one has gone through a conceptualizational development. Then it is remarked that, as a result, one's perspective on moral matters has changed. Consequently, earlier forms of moral reasoning are now considered less adequate. That is, they are either rejected by now, or at least judged to be insufficient. The conclusion is, finally, that the development implies an improvement.[15]

In three different ways the *internal* justification of the developmental claim is thus dependent on the development that is to be justified. In the first place, the justification actually is only possible at all as a result of the development that it is about. No justification can be given until after some conceptual development. No evaluative comparison between specific stages can be made until after both stages have been reached or passed through. Moreover, the particular form of justification is only made possible by the fact that the stage of which it is typical has been attained. In this way the development to be justified is a prerequisite of the justification of that development.

Secondly, and more important, it is also the development itself that (so to say) produces the *reasons* that are used in the justification, for the justification of the developmental claim also is based, logically, on *the specific characteristics of the last stage* (or at least of the stage which is considered to be more adequate than its precursor). It is precisely because of the specific properties of this new stage that the developmental claim is made, and it is precisely with reference to these properties that the claim is justified.

Thirdly, not only is the justification of the evaluative claim based on these new facts, that are given with the new developmental stage, but *also the criterion, used in the evaluation of these new facts, is derived from the insights that are given with the new developmental stage.* This is so because, as I have been trying to show, the new stage brings forth a new and qualitatively different perspective on the domain of morality. The new conception of morality implies a *new standard* according to which from now on moral stages are compared.

Thus, in each new stage the justification of the moral developmental claim is based on *new facts* that are weighed in the light of *new criteria*, which are both typical of that new stage. In each new stage there is a new conception of morality, issuing not only in a new way of dealing with moral problems, but also in a new way of evaluating and justifying moral development. And if our suggestion above is right, then perhaps in some or all stages there is a new form of *justification* as well.

So here is an interesting relation between genesis and justification, which is not easy to grasp. From an observer perspective, we can never derive from the pure facts about the developmental process in question sufficient reasons for the evaluation thereof. That would inevitably land us into a naturalistic or genetic fallacy.[16] But I, as an actor and as a developing person, can as a result of this development (which is accomplished in constant interaction with other actors), have gained new insights, in the framework of which I can have good *reasons* (which I did not have before) to evaluate things in a new way. I can also now evaluate my own (pattern of) development in a new way. And, in this case, part of my reasoning will be precisely derived from the particular character of the newly acquired stage, whereas another essential part of my reasoning is inherent in the foundations of morality that are typical for that same new stage. Thus, although the development 'produces' the reasons, in the sense indicated above, the mere fact that I developed (or my own descriptive developmental claim about it) can never by itself be a sufficient reason to endorse any evaluative developmental claim.[17] On the other hand, however, the fact that my having those reasons and my now finding them the best possible reasons is a result of my own psychological development does not by itself make me vulnerable to any reproach of genetic fallacy. If there are other people who can accept those reasons as valid – people who are therefore by definition in the same developmental stage – we may for the time being have arrived at the best possible argument.

4 Implications for the justification of moral education

So far, I have been trying to elucidate some rather far-reaching implications of interpreting moral development as a conceptualizational development through qualitatively different stages. Are we thus condemned to relativism? I think we are not, or at least not to an intolerable form of relativism, but there are serious consequences. I will first spell out some of the implications, and then see if we can mitigate them to a certain degree.

First of all, clearly there can be no absolute justification or foundation of morality according to cognitive structuralist theory. Each justification is relative to, and fundamentally dependent on, a certain stage or form of moral reasoning. This is also true with respect to what is now usually regarded as the highest stage of moral development. However, to those who gave up the search for ultimate justifications of moral principles altogether, it may be something of a relief that we might be able to distinguish a *limited number* of qualitatively different justificational systems, and at least find reasons to consider the one *better than* another. This kind of *relative justification* may be the best we can hope for, and is perhaps not so poor after all.

Secondly, we may notice that the idea of qualitatively and essentially different moral stages need not imply that they are *totally* different. There may be components that do not change over some or all of the stages. Yet, the fundamental perspectives *do* alter, and with them the basic forms of conceptual coherence.

The main point that may contribute to the overcoming of extreme forms of relativism, however, is that developmental stages are not entirely incomparable systems of thought because we are talking about a development which we ourselves have gone through, and which in that sense is not completely strange to us, although we have left the earlier stages behind. We have lived through the stages that we are comparing: we have been on the inside of them. That is to say, *in so far as* we share a common developmental past, we may come to an agreement about interpretations, evaluations and justifications of the distinct forms of moral reasoning and the respective developmental claims. In case of disagreement, we may go back in history, looking for a common point of departure from where the argument can be set up with regard to later stages.

Difficulties will mainly arise where there is no shared past. In general, this will be the case as soon as ramifications appear in developmental paths. Curiously, hardly any developmental theory allows for this possibility – which is certainly due to the biological background of the paradigm. I will not go into this possibility here.[18] The other case in which a common history is lacking, however, is directly relevant to our purpose. If within the same developmental pattern the difference between a child and its educator – by definition – amounts to at least one stage, and if we take the notion of stages in the strict sense specified above, then we will have to accept that in their relationship justifications cannot really be given except in terms of the developmental stage of the least advanced. This implies that *to the person who is to be educated a justification of current educational aims cannot be given.* For then, by definition, he cannot yet have a sufficient insight into the specific *perspective* on morality which is characteristic of a later stage he is supposed to attain in his further development and which lies at the root of the justification. The adult can see the earlier stages he has passed through as part of the way to his actual stage. But the child does not in the same way have sufficient access to his potential later stages. Moral education can be justified to co-educators (parents, teachers, counsellors) but not to the child concerned.

Is such a conclusion acceptable? Is it acceptable, particularly if we realize that justification is an intrinsic part of our concept of morality; and that, as I have said before, an important aspect of moral education should be accomplished precisely in, and through, the mutual adducing of reasons for what we think and do – including in moral education? Or do we have to abandon the basic notion of qualitatively different stages which is so important in cognitive structuralistic theory? Have I been sharpening the model beyond measure? I think that I have only made explicit what really is an inherent problem. To me it seems unwarranted to relinquish the cognitive structuralistic approach for this reason, because it is the only model that in an inspiring way theoretically accounts for and sufficiently captures the aspect of moral *development*. Moreover, the theory has been confirmed pretty well in recent research (cf. e.g. Thornton and Thornton, 1983). Therefore, I will, accepting this basic approach, now try to mitigate my conclusions. I will mention four points.

In the first place, although we may admit the impossibility of a direct justification to the child, in moral education one has always to face a potential demand for it later on: namely *ex post facto*, when the child has grown up and reached the developmental stage of the educator. This future potentiality may certainly affect the actual relationship between the child and the adult. Moreover, if the child goes through more than two stages – as virtually all developmental theories posit – there may be *a growing and deepening relationship of trust*, in which the child reposes confidence in measures that he cannot sufficiently understand, and yet accepts because of his appreciation of the role (and possibly the justification) of the educator in earlier developmental stages. The educator in turn accepts the child's confidence partly because he knows that in principle he can *ex post facto* justify what is now being accepted blindly.[19]

5 Justification in moral education

The foregoing does not, indeed, alter the conclusion that we cannot justify our actual moral education to the child. That would require the child's understanding and accepting (at level II) of the moral perspective of the educator and thereby at least in this respect remove the need for moral education. Apparently, all we can do is to give reasons (at level I) in terms of the stage the child is at. Must we therefore conclude that there can be no *educational* value in the asking and giving of reasons? I do not think this should be our conclusion, and that is my second point. In each (Kohlbergian) stage the child makes certain choices, accompanied by some sort of reasoning. At first, such deliberations may be rather crude and rudimentary. But in deliberating and talking about, for instance, how toys or cookies should be distributed, the child learns to search for reasons and to exchange them. In this interchange, more typically conventional reasons may come up, and it is only on this basis that eventually the sort of autonomous principled reasoning may gradually emerge, that *we* consider an essential aspect of morality. During this whole process, as I stressed before, the idea of justification itself develops accordingly. But whatever the differences between the stages, the giving and asking for reasons can be practised and exercised all along. And in this respect it is the educator who can set the example. It is a *practice* into which the child is to be initiated step by step and into which he can be initiated from the first stage of moral development on.

What in this process is learned, is primarily *that* reasons should be given, *that* the question why and wherefore should be answered. Only in the second place does the child learn to think about *what* sorts of answers may be considered adequate. In this respect the justification of moral education itself may have a function as well, even if this has another meaning for the educator or the parent than it has for the child, and even if the child cannot properly understand the arguments given. I do not, incidentally, want to suggest that 'content' (what the reasons are *about*) is not important. Moral education, of course, starts from content. But in going through the deliberations about concrete ideas on how things ought to be done, a person may come to criticize the foundations of his moral convictions and judgements as well. A child may, firmly sitting on the shoulders of his father, protest against nuclear weapons. Yet the foundations of his protest will be rather different from those of his father. The child in fact protests because of his alliance to his father, whereas the father's protest – perhaps – is based on an autonomous choice of specific moral principles.[20] Content is important, for sure, but – and this is particularly clear in the cognitive structuralistic approach – content is not enough.

My third point is related to this. I have stressed that justification is intrinsically connected to our concept of morality. But advisedly I said, justification is part of *our* concept of morality. Our concept of morality and our concept of justification are not the same as the child's, however. It is only in the later (Kohlbergian) stages that justification in the sense of giving adequate reasons for what we think and do gradually becomes an *intrinsic* part of our notion of morality. As a consequence, we, adults or parents, may consider certain forms of justification to the child obligatory which the child itself does not conceive that way at all. He does not miss the kinds of reasoning that we feel to be indispensable. In this regard too, the child has yet to be initiated gradually into a practice and into a conceptualization of that practice, by which he will come to adopt finally the criteria according to which we act.

This brings me to my fourth and last point. Surely in moral education and as part of moral education we will have to justify what we say and what we do including what we may say about (moral) education itself. But in doing so, we must realize that there may be forms of misapprehension on the way that are *essential*. For we *anticipate* conditions which have not in fact been realized yet, conditions which *will become effective precisely by our anticipating them*. This sounds rather profound, but it actually is what is being done in normal moral education all along. That we are not aware of it most of the time is only because the qualitatively different stages in moral development are *conceptualizational* stages. The disenchanting conclusion, therefore, is that in moral education we should proceed rather much as we have always been doing as a matter of course – only now being more aware of the conceptual differences between the child and ourselves, and of the implications thereof.

That in moral education we can get along well with children even if in terms of our own notion of justification, is just one instance of our dealing with children from our own different-from-theirs conceptual framework most of the time. The same words, we may now realize, are used for sometimes quite different moral conceptions functioning in quite different conceptual configurations. Yet in moral education we use those words, and we will have to *continue* to do so. In giving an example, we may realize now that examples may be understood in rather different ways. Yet in moral education we will have to *continue* to set the example. In trying to develop the child's virtuousness, we must know that the general idea of virtue and the concepts of the various virtues may be different in several respects.[21] Yet in moral education we will have to *continue* to

36

further virtuousness. In short, the educator, from his higher developmental stage, will have to set the example, to ask for reasons, to further the development of the virtues. The educator who is aware of the fundamental differences in the way moral reality is conceptualized, will have to do these things all the same – but from a better understanding of the educational situation, resulting in a well-informed and tolerant appreciation of the sometimes radical conceptual differences between the child's understanding and his own. This will conduce to a better command of the subtleties of moral education in which *justification* plays such an important role: sometimes starting from the child's developmental stage, sometimes carefully extending justificatory strategies to a one-stage-above approach, sometimes also unreservedly arguing from the educator's own moral perspective – but always at the same time from a serious understanding of the essential forms of misunderstanding that will be necessarily involved.

Notes

1 Of course, I do not mean that they are necessarily or always being done separately.
2 Or, if it is our own action, we intend it in a certain way.
3 In principle, *two* such stages are sufficient to speak of qualitative development.
4 An evaluative developmental claim always presupposes a descriptive developmental claim, because the evaluation concerns first and foremost the developmental pattern referred to in the descriptive claim.
5 Conceptualizational development as a rule will not leave unaffected the interpretation or reconstruction of the foregoing stages of level I. Each new mode of conceptualizing may bring along its own view of the past. For this reason I have numbered the various stages in schema II; $S(n)$, $S(n-1)$, $S(n-2)$, . . . instead of $S(1)$, $S(2)$, $S(3)$, ...
6 Kohlberg rightly emphasizes that in the earliest stages there is no clear-cut moral dimension apart from, for example, the dimension of social development. And, as in conceptualizational development, the moral dimension becomes more independent,

it will on the other hand need to keep its connections with other domains of life. As for that it is a question of how far there can be such a thing as specifically *moral* education.

7 The two general requirements specified here are necessary for any theory of *conceptualizational* development, including theories of collective development (e.g. cultural development, scientific development); (cf. Van Haaften *et al.*, 1986).

8 Two forms of *cumulation* should be distinguished here. On the one hand, in S(n) the arguments and criteria of S(n-1) may be accepted as *valid but insufficient*. In this case, in each new stage the judgements at level I are considered more adequate because they *comply* with more criteria at level II. On the other hand, in S(n) the arguments and criteria of S(n-1) may be rejected as *invalid*. In that case, in each new stage the judgements at level I are considered more adequate because they satisfy *other* criteria at level II that are by then regarded as better criteria for the dimension in question. Social development seems to be of the first kind; moral development rather of the second.

9 The question here is, what is to be considered as a new and qualitatively different *form* or *structure* of conceptualization (including a new form or structure of reasoning). We may, as in structuralism, take a structure to be the totality of specific connections between all relevant elements of a particular system (cf. also Flavell, 1982). Such structures could not possibly be known by the developing person. In this sense he does not know the actual stage he is 'at', and much less his earlier stages. The specific structure in the above-mentioned sense of a conceptualizational system, as distinguished at level II, however, is determined by a few *basic insights* that leaven all judgements of level I. Perhaps it is primarily these basic insights that are compared when stages are evaluated.

10 These stage-criteria are formulated *in abstracto*. They are not, of course, intended as a description of criteria that are actually used by, for instance, Kohlberg. On the other hand, *if* these criteria were to be accepted, it is questionable whether all Kohlberg's stages would indeed satisfy them.

11 For the reason given in note 9, for a person to have reached stage (n) it should not be required that he is able to anticipate *all* of its implications. He must understand and accept its characteristic basic insights, which means that he does understand the implications thereof in at least some regards.

12 Both actor and observer must themselves have reached the highest stage that they are talking about, for otherwise they would not be able to compare that stage to another one in the required sense. More about the relation between actor perspective and observer perspective and the justifications of both of them can be found in Van Haaften *et al.* (1986).

13 The *term* 'justification' is ambiguous over process and product. Moreover, it can be used both for the serious giving of reasons, and in a more restricted sense for when the reasons given are also considered *sufficient* or decisive. But the boundaries are not always clear, and I have not tried to distinguish consistently the term in those respects.

14 Not necessarily need we ourselves have gone through the development that we describe and evaluate. To a certain degree we can and do sometimes judge forms of conceptualizational development that are more or less strange to us.

15 In short, reasons are given why earlier forms of moral reasoning should be considered inadequate or insufficient. This leaves open *what* these reasons might be. They need, for instance, not be cumulative over the stages. The fact that $S(n)$ could not come about but on the basis of $S(n-1)$ and in that regard presupposes its predecessor, does not imply that the *reasons* to prefer $S(n)$ to $S(n-1)$ should include the reasons why $S(n-1)$ was preferred to $S(n-2)$. In general, it may be better not to specify in advance what sorts of reasons might count as sufficient in order to justify developmental claims. There can be several (cf. e.g. Flavell, 1972). Moreover, it is not very clear what is meant by often proposed candidates like 'hierarchical integration'. Should stage n *logically* presuppose stage $(n-1)$? And precisely in what sense 'logically' (cf. Locke, 1986)? Must stage (n) be more *consistent* than stage $(n-)$? But in what sense 'more consistent'? Perhaps the stages need not each time be distinguished and evaluated by the same kind of criteria. I have argued (Van Haaften, 1984) that at least *one* transition between stages can be defended by means of a transcendental argument.

16 In general, relevant facts are always necessary but at the same time can never be sufficient to justify an evaluative claim.

17 By definition, if a person has reached a new stage, he will have new reasons for his (moral) judgements. But the converse is not true, of course: a person's having new reasons does not *imply* that he has reached a new stage.

18 It is interesting to note that Kohlberg, who has done so much to turn Piaget's interactionistic model of development into a really *intersubjective* form of interactionism, hardly seems to consider this possibility of branching. In point of fact, it rather would require explanation that there should *not* be any furcations in developmental paths in conceptualizational development.

19 This point of *ex post facto justification* is important for another reason. Adults, justifying moral education between them, could in principle (for instance in a conventionalistic stage) resort to a purely technological concept of education, in which the child is nothing more than the 'object' of their 'measures'. In a justification *ex post facto* of one adult to another the former child will have to be conceived as a 'subject' as well.

20 I owe the example to G. Snik.

21 Our notion of virtue is different in the various stages of moral development. Moreover, our appreciation of virtues is not stage-independent. Some virtues are desirable only in certain stages and rather undesirable in other stages, as for instance Slote (1983) has argued in respect of 'life-planfulness'. But even with regard to the 'permanent' virtues we should be aware of fundamentally different interpretations and appreciations in the consecutive stages, as has been shown, for example, by Kohlberg with regard to 'justice'.

References

Bickhard, M.H. (1978). The Nature of Developmental Stages. *Human Development*, 21, 217–33.

Boyd, D.R. (1986). The Oughts of Is: Kohlberg at the Interface between Moral Philosophy and Developmental Psychology. *In* S. Modgil and C. Modgil (eds), *Lawrence Kohlberg. Consensus and Controversy*. Philadelphia and London.

Brainerd, C. (1978). The Stage Question in Cognitive-Developmental Theory. *The Behavioral and Brain Sciences*, 2, 173–213.

Flavell, J.H. (1972). An Analysis of Cognitive-Developmental Sequences. *Genetic Psychology Monographs*, 86, 279–350.

Flavell, J.H. (1982). Structures, Stages, and Sequences in Cognitive Development. *In* W.A. Collins (ed.), *The Concept of Development* (Minnesota Symposia on Child Psychology, Vol. 15), pp. 1–28. Hillsdale, NJ, Lawrence Erlbaum Associates.

Haaften, A.W. van (1984). Een ontwikkelingstheoretische bena-
dering van de 'is-ought question'. (A developmental approach to
the is-ought question.) *Pedagogische Studiën,* 61, 272–81.
Haaften, A.W. van, Korthals, M., Widdershoven, G.A.M., de Mul, J.
and Snik, G.L.M. (1986). *Ontwikkelingsfilosofie. Een onderzoek
naar grondslagen van ontwikkeling en opvoeding.* (Philosophy of
Development. An Inquiry into Foundations of Development and
Education.) Muiderberg.
Habermas, J. (1981). *Theorie des kommunikativen Handelns,* 2 Vols.
Frankfurt/Main.
Kant, I. (1781). *Kritik der reinen Vernunft.*
Kohlberg, L. (1969). Stage and Sequence: The Cognitive-Develop-
mental Approach to Socialization. *In* G. Goslin (ed.), *Handbook
of Socialization,* pp. 347–480.
Kohlberg, L. (1976). Moral Stages and Moralization, the Cognitive
Developmental Approach. *In* Th. Lickona (ed.), *Moral Develop-
ment and Behaviour. Theory, Research and Social Issues.* New
York.
Kohlberg, L. (1981). *The Philosophy of Moral Development. Essays
on Moral Development, Vol. I.* San Francisco.
Kohlberg, L. (1984). *The Psychology of Moral Development. Essays on
Moral Development, Vol. II.* San Francisco.
Kohlberg, L., Levine, C. and Hewer, A. (1983). *Moral Stages: A
Current Formulation and a Response to Critics.* Basel.
Locke, D. 1986. A Psychologist among the Philosophers: Philo-
sophical Aspects of Kohlberg's Theories. *In* S. Modgil and
C. Modgil (eds), *Lawrence Kohlberg. Consensus and Controversy*
Philadelphia/London.
Longeot, F. (1978). *Les stades operatives de Piaget et des facteurs de
l'intelligence.* Grenoble.
Modgil, S. and Modgil, C. (eds) (1986). *Lawrence Kohlberg.
Consensus and Controversy.* Philadelphia/London.
Piaget, J. (1932). *Le jugement moral chez l'enfant.* Paris.
Piaget, J. (1960). The General Problem of the Psychological Develop-
ment of the Child. *In* J.M. Tanner and B. Inhelder (eds), *A
Consideration of the Biological, Psychological, and Cultural
Approaches to the Understanding of Human Development and
Behavior,* Vol. IV. New York.
Piaget, J. and Inhelder, B. (1969). *The Psychology of the Child.*
London.
Rest, J. (1973). Patterns of Preference and Comprehension in Moral

Judgment. *Journal of Personality*, **41**, 86–109.

Rest, J. (1976). New Approaches in the Assessment of Moral Judgment. *In* Th. Lickona (ed.), *Moral Development and Behavior. Theory, Research and Social Issues.* New York.

Slote, M. (1983). *Goods and Virtues.* Oxford.

Thornton, D. and Thornton, S. (1983). Structure, Content, and the Direction of Development in Kohlberg's Theory. *In* H. Weinreich-Haste and D. Locke (eds), *Morality in the Making. Thought, Action, and the Social Context.* Chichester/New York.

Vuyk, R. (1981). *Piaget's Genetic Epistemology 1965–1980.* London.

Education and the moral emotions

BEN SPIECKER

1   Introduction

Moral philosophers and psychologists such as R.M. Hare and
L. Kohlberg have often been reproached for giving insufficient
attention to the question of which moral emotions may be
found in a 'decent' or moral human being (Williams, 1973:
207).[1] It seems to me that this reproach is justified and the
neglect is particularly felt in the field of moral education. The
capacity for experiencing moral emotions – e.g. guilt – is a
necessary condition for being a moral person. We feel entitled
to blame someone for not feeling repentance after wilfully
harming someone else.

But can we educate moral emotions? Nowadays it is often
said that our emotions can be distinguished from each other,
and justified, on the basis of their cognitive–evaluative
component.[2] And because these evaluations can be influenced,
the phrase 'education of emotions' is not a contradiction in
terms. Moral emotions are taught; if a child breaks the rules it
learns not only *that* (or *why*) it should feel guilty, but also (as its
parents make clear) *what* feeling guilty means. The child learns
a whole range of what is considered *proper* behaviour – from
'don't look so insolent' and 'go and apologize' to correct

attitudes toward an offence: 'You should feel terrible about what you've done' (cf. Arman-Jones, 1985: 9).

The rational tradition (Kant, Piaget, Kohlberg) has made its influence strongly felt in the field of moral education and development; in this tradition moral learning is not considered to be a matter of supplying missing emotions and motives, but of developing our innate intellectual capacities. According to this conception, education initiates the child into the forms of knowledge. Matters such as attachments, tendencies and character receive less attention (White, 1984). However, in order to maintain a well-ordered and just society, it is precisely these ties, moral sentiments and motives that are of decisive importance.

In this article, I want to explore further the question of what we understand by moral emotions and sentiments and in what way these can be influenced or educated. I shall distinguish two subclasses of moral emotions, and subsequently examine in more detail their *logical* and *developmental–psychological* relations to one another. In conclusion, I will make a number of observations about the discussion between L. Kohlberg and G. Gilligan, because I think that their controversy can be illuminated by means of the subclasses of moral emotions that have been distinguished.

There are no clear classification-criteria which distinguish (moral) emotions from attitudes, motives or traits of character. Most emotions and motives are also regarded as virtues and vices – e.g. envy, benevolence and lust (Peters, 1974: 182; see also Rorty, 1980). Some emotions are by nature motivational – feelings of obligation, regard or respect for a moral principle in the case of conscientiousness – and form an integral part of certain virtues. Virtues, and thus vices as well, include both specific wants and feelings. If we say of someone that his character is friendly or sympathetic, then we also imply that this person is capable of having certain feelings and emotions (e.g. tenderness). The same applies to the term 'attitude'; a moral attitude (e.g. respect for persons) logically implies certain emotions and feelings (Dent, 1984: 16). Thus, two types of virtues, called by D. Hume the 'natural' and the 'artificial', correspond to the two subclasses of moral emotions which I will distinguish.

2 Two subclasses of moral emotions

What do we consider to belong to the category of moral emotions? We could ask whether moral emotions are distinguished from other emotions by specific manifestations of behaviour or characteristic sensations (cf. Richards, 1971: 250). Neither case is satisfactory; one's face can turn red as a result of either shame or anger, warmth or exertion. Nor do physical sensations form a necessary condition for moral emotions to occur or be distinguished. The physical sensation of anger, for example, will differ from case to case: a dry mouth, shaking hands, a pounding heart. On the other hand, the explanation a person gives for experiencing a moral emotion *is* characteristic of one subclass of moral emotions. Among other things, this explanation implies that the person thinks he has broken a moral rule or principle, or is intending to do so, and is, moreover, of the opinion that there are no excusing conditions. For instance, I can feel guilty when I wilfully treat someone else unkindly or deliberately break a promise. In turn, I feel indignant when someone else fails to keep a promise. Moral emotions which result from consciously transgressing a moral principle should disappear after the relationship with the other(s) has been re-established. Reconciliation can be effected by confessing guilt, by showing regret, by asking for forgiveness, and so on. That some moral emotions are logically dependent on the conviction that moral rules or principles are applicable to us can be explained by comparing the emotions 'shame' and 'embarrassment' (Bedford, 1967: 85). The behaviour of a person who feels embarrassed will often not differ greatly from that of someone who feels ashamed; nevertheless, both find themselves in different situations. Moral shame occurs when someone breaks a moral standard; a necessary condition for the correctness of a statement such as 'she is ashamed of herself' is that the person in question feels

45

that she has acted wrongly. This person can be blamed because she can be held responsible. On the other hand, a person can be embarrassed both without his knowledge and without his responsibility. For the behaviour of small children who have been put under our responsibility, we can probably feel both shame and embarrassment.

One can, on the basis of the above, draw the conclusion that there is a subclass of *moral* emotions, of which a necessary condition is formed by the awareness that moral rules apply to oneself and to others and that in some cases these rules are broken. But breaking a moral rule in one's actions or experiencing immoral emotions – immoral emotions (malice) can also call up moral emotions (indignation) – does not in itself form a sufficient condition, as it is possible that a person deliberately goes against moral principles without experiencing moral emotions. I will call this subclass of moral emotions (moral) *rule*-emotions. With this type of moral emotions the cognitive evaluation consists of considering a moral rule or principle to be applicable to oneself and to others.

Moral rule-emotions are thus connected with moral rules, and only a person who has mastered these rules can have these emotions. These *rule*-emotions are rational: for, in principle, a person can explain and justify why he experiences these emotions.

I have already touched on the relationship between moral emotions and virtues. Rule-emotions correspond to, or are a part of, what are called the 'artificial' or non-teleological virtues or traits of character (reasonableness, justice). The non-teleologically virtuous person experiences and acts on the basis of these motivating rule-emotions; he shows respect for the moral law, he feels obligated to keep his promise, or, formulated more generally, he has a predilection for justice (Steutel, 1986). The bearer of artificial virtues cares about moral rules, he has acquired the disposition of a positive commitment to moral rules and is inclined to evaluate certain conflicts and situations with the help of these rules.

I come now to the second type of moral emotions, the *altruistic* emotions, sometimes called 'natural attitudes'. The moral character of these altruistic emotions is not always sufficiently recognized – this may be the result of a 'genetic fallacy'. Owing to the fact that the instinctive wants and urges of young children have to be socialized, the attitudes and moral emotions of adults are wrongly taken to be a mere masking of these natural urges (cf. MacIntyre, 1967).

In developmental psychology, actions motivated by altruism are often taken as a form of 'pro-social behaviour', as actions that are intended to aid or benefit another person or group without the actor's anticipation of external rewards (Mussen and Eisenberg-Berg, 1977: 3). The operationalization of this concept frequently comes down to 'helping behaviour' or 'compliance' (see Wispé, 1978; Bridgeman, 1983). But from a conceptual point of view, not all helping behaviour is altruistic; if an attractive student stopped me on the campus and asked for my name, I would probably give it to her, but not because I felt altruistic (Krebs, 1978: 143–4).

Altruistic emotions, such as feelings of compassion, concern, generosity and sympathy, are directed at other people (or animals) specifically in the light of their weal and woe (cf. Schopenhauer, 1840; Blum, 1980). In particular, parents and educators stress the importance of these altruistic emotions explicitly when speaking of the aims of education and the future of their children. Parents hope and strive to have their children grow up to have a good character and to become pleasant, trustworthy and compassionate persons, who know how to love and who have enough friends (cf. Peters, 1974: 331; White, 1984). The so-called 'natural' (or teleological) virtues are also formed by helping the child to acquire altruistic emotions.

The central altruistic emotions are directed at those fellow human beings who find themselves in misery, who are in distress, or who suffer; they are 'moral' in that they involve a regard for the good of other persons (feelings of pity) (cf. Schopenhauer).[3] These emotions have a cognitive component as well: it does make some difference whether the other feels embarrassed or is suffering. The content of the cognition, however, does not in itself form a sufficient condition for speaking of an altruistic emotion. An element of feeling should also be involved: one should be '(painfully) struck' or 'touched' by the distress of the other. Nevertheless, there is no question of one 'typical' feeling; concern for another person (or animal) can involve feelings of shock, hope and (afterwards) relief, in which the component of physical sensations can also make itself felt.

Altruistic emotions are to be distinguished from moods (excitement, elation, depression) and from personal feelings (admiration, respect); neither being in a good mood nor being fond of a person forms a necessary condition for having altruistic emotions. When I am in a bad mood I can still feel pity for a neighbour who is in trouble, even though I dislike the neighbour.

On what grounds now can the distinction between rule-emotions and altruistic emotions be justified? Up to this point I have not got beyond making the distinction between observing the *condition* of other persons in the light of their weal and woe on the one hand and judging a person's *actions* (or one's own) by a moral principle on the other hand. Rule-emotions presuppose that an action is judged with the aid of a moral rule. Because the judgement is based on a rule, one may expect to find that persons involved in identical situations in which rules are broken have the same rule-emotion(s); if X and Y are both witnesses to Z's theft, one can reasonably expect both X and Y to be indignant about the offence.

In altruistic emotions, a judgement based on a moral rule does not form a necessary condition for experiencing these emotions. Nowadays, as the psychologist R.B. Zajonc observes, emotions are all too often considered as exclusively *post*-cognitive, i.e. occurring only after considerable cognitive operations have been completed. Against this view, Zajonc argues that we cannot be introduced to a person without experiencing an immediate feeling of attraction or repulsion, though we may completely fail to notice the other person's hair colour: 'But seldom do we escape the reaction that the other person impressed us as pleasant or unpleasant, as nice or irritating' (1980: 153, 156).[4]

Compassion, friendliness and helpfulness presuppose only that one reacts to certain characteristics of a situation or to the condition of the other, i.e. that one recognizes or understands that someone else needs help, and that this perception leads one to undertake charitable actions. Forming a judgement is no necessary condition, as is being sensitive, being receptive to the weal and woe of the other. The friendly or caring person does not as a rule act in order to be virtuous; he is rarely aware that he acts morally (Blum, 1980). In order to justify his altruistic emotion, it is not necessary for a person to call upon a moral rule. If X, filled with care, hurries to help Y, X does not necessarily need to be convinced that he is acting in accordance with a general reason or principle. An altruistic emotion and the corresponding wish to watch over or promote the other's well-being, or to lighten his suffering, can be justified by referring to the weal and woe of the other, to his situation or condition which 'strikes' us. Depending on the result of the intervention, acting out of compassion is characterized by, among other things, feelings of pleasure, relief, joy ('a load off our minds'), sadness or frustration. If altruistic emotions are to occur, a necessary condition is also formed by the perception and understanding that all is 'not well' with the other(s). This does not of course rule out the possibility that perception and understanding can *also* be influenced by a moral rule; X is worried about Y because Y is, in his actions, less and less concerned with moral principles.

In my opinion, the distinction between both subclasses can also be further elucidated with the help of two types of duties, called *perfect* and *imperfect* duties by Kant and 'Rechts-' and 'Tugend-' or 'Liebespflichten' by Schopenhauer (Kant, 1978: 87; Schopenhauer, 1979: 57, 110, 125). Perfect or 'Rechts-' duties are those duties which do not allow an exception in favour of an impulse; these duties not only state what we may not or may never do – do not steal, kill, lie – they also, when the rules are transgressed, compel us to undergo those emotions which I have earlier called rule-emotions. The altruistic emotions, on the other hand, are connected with the imperfect duties or 'Liebespflichten', in which there are no rules which concretely dictate when we should do what or which altruistic emotions we should experience. We will show differential reactions to transgressions of the two types of duties. Unjustly not showing rule-emotions will be considered a *'vice'* ('Laster'); failing in the altruistic emotions will be understood as a 'lack of virtue' ('Untugend') (cf. Nunner-Winkler, 1984: 349).

The altruistic emotions form part of the 'natural' (or teleological) virtues. The bearer of these 'natural' virtues is characterized by the disposition of a positive commitment to the fate of his fellow man (Steutel, 1986). The motivating emotions of this person are interwoven with the perception of, and sometimes with the judgement of, the weal and woe of the other. In his actions, he strives after a certain aim (*telos*) – to abolish the sufferings of fellow man.

To distinguish both subclasses from a logical point of view may sound plausible, but the question of how children acquire these emotions is of completely different order. I will attempt to prove that in the development of a child both types of moral emotions influence each other in such a way that, on the one hand, the altruistic emotions form, from a *developmental-psychological* point of view a condition for acquiring the rule-emotions, while on the other hand (the development of) the *justification* of the altruistic emotions, the degree to which they are *proper*, is influenced by rule-emotions. Finally, I will explore the issue of (the development of) the *justification* of the moral rule-emotions.

3 The development of moral emotions

In the development of a child, the elementary altruistic emotions appear first; this type of moral emotions have primacy from an *ontogenetic* point of view.[5] Small children are quickly touched by the cries of pain and sorrow of other living beings. Their empathic capacities are not yet 'corrected' by cognitive evaluations. The infant is not yet capable of making a subject–object distinction; it does not yet have a (complete) concept of 'person'. Given the limited cognitive abilities, a number of emotion-terms cannot as yet be applied to the infant; we do call these children 'friendly' but not (yet) 'charitable', they are 'teasing', but not 'malicious' (cf. Arman-Jones, 1985).

I assume that learning either type of moral emotions will be made possible to a large degree by *identical* pedagogical conditions. For a child the learning process consists of acquiring moral rules and concepts about acts such as promising and comforting, traits such as honesty and faithfulness, and emotions such as indignation and sorrow. Adults stimulate these learning processes by encouraging children to imagine themselves in the position of another (role-taking opportunities) and by pointing out to children, in their pedagogical procedures, what the results of their actions are ('inductive discipline'). Because the altruistic emotions are primary in ontogenetic perspective, I will examine the development of these moral emotions. In doing so I will pay particular attention to the works of the developmental psychologist M.L. Hoffman.

Learning altruistic emotions presupposes that infants have a 'cognitive sense of others'. At the end of the first year of life they attain person permanence and become aware of others as physical entities distinct from themselves; a year later they have become vaguely aware that others have their own feelings and thoughts. In as much as a young child does not yet have a sense of others as separate entities, it experiences the distress of others as its own unpleasant feelings. According to Hoffman, we can, in this case, speak of a precursor of empathy or of an involuntary 'global empathy'. As the acquisition of language progresses, the child will be more capable of identifying the emotions of others, and its role-taking capability will increase.

How does the developmental shift take place from one's personal empathic distress to a concern for the victim, to a feeling of compassion or sympathetic distress? According to Hoffman it is reasonable to assume that the experience of an unpleasant effect includes the wish or motive that it be

51

terminated. Such a motive is then transferred to other persons (Hoffman, 1984a: 116, 1984a). Hoffman does not explain exactly how this transference takes place; he characterizes the infant too much as a solitary explorer of the social environment, and thus takes too little account of the *pedagogical* context. Is it not much more plausible that a child's acquisition of elementary feeling of sympathy can be understood because of the specific relationship (a relationship *sui generis*) which these children often have with their caretakers? Is it not this early parent–child relationship in particular that is often characterized specifically by a wealth of altruistic emotions flowing from the caretakers? Where else do we often see the whole range of altruistic emotions but in those cases in which the adults who feel responsible for them act as loving and caring 'double-agents' (J. Shotter) of the needs and interests of babies and infants. The adult voices the child's needs and interests, and interprets its actions as expressions of feelings and emotions (hunger, pain, happiness), and subsequently reacts to these in a caring manner. The shift from empathic distress to sympathetic distress described takes place, one could say, only if a young child has been taken up in a network of actions motivated by altruistic emotions.

As a result of its empathic capacity the child learns what the consequences of its actions are for others and also that it feels sad or guilty if it hurts others. According to Hoffman, it is of great importance to point out to a child the inner condition of others in forming the empathic capacities and the altruistic emotions.

> The experiences are exemplified by the parent's use of inductive discipline, which calls attention to the pain or injury caused by the child's action or encourages the child to imagine how it would feel to be in the victim's place. Third, we expect role-taking opportunities in positive contexts to help sharpen the child's cognitive sense of others and increase the likelihood that they will pay attention to others, thus extending their empathic capability (Hoffman, 1984b: 290).

By using this inductive discipline technique, however, the child is at the same time also informed about the moral rule or norm 'considering others'. Besides indicating harmful consequences of the child's action for the other, inductive discipline often also communicates the moral rules the parents adhere to. In these inductions parents also show and motivate their rule-emotions, which supports the conjecture that the development of rule-emotions becomes possible by virtue of altruistic emotions.

That a child only acquires the rule-emotions if it does not have a disturbed bond or relationship with adults is an assertion which is often heard. A child only has 'authority guilt' when it trusts a caretaker, when it is attached to, and scared of losing the care and love of, the 'significant other'. The absence of certain moral feeling or emotions sometimes is evidence of the absence of certain 'natural attachments' (Rawls, 1972: 486). For the sake of its relationship with its parents or caretakers the child will be inclined to confess its faults and to seek reconciliation. All this presupposes, however, that a young child has an (elementary) capacity for empathy; it must be able to feel or perceive the feelings (happiness, anger) of the parents. Moral *rule-emotions seem to be able to come into being only on the basis of the elementary altruistic emotions*, such as fellow-feelings or sympathy.

Educators also call upon the altruistic emotions in forming the 'artificial' virtues corresponding to the rule-emotions. As has been said before, the moral agent is characterized by a positive attitude towards moral rules, and this means that she is dedicated to these rules in a benevolent, upright and loyal manner. Educators not only try to teach children to act according to moral rules and conventions, they also want them to do so with 'heart and soul' and 'in the right spirit'. They teach children the rule 'stealing is wrong' by pointing out to them that they also do not enjoy losing things they are attached to, and that they would also be angry or sad in such cases. In short, educators call upon feelings of sympathy and upon fellow-feelings in forming 'artificial' virtues as well. A moral person seldom acts only from feelings of 'pure' duty to rules. If a person says she feels obliged to do something, then in many cases she also indicates that this feeling of duty involves altruistic emotions. If I worry about a sick friend, feelings of care and compassion make me feel obligated to go and see that person (cf. Neblett, 1981: 17).

4 The justification of moral emotions

After having touched on the influence of altruistic emotions in forming rule-emotions, in the form of a *condition of genesis*, I will now examine the influence the opposite way around. Altruistic emotions can be *justified*, and *corrected*, with the help of rule-emotions; rule-emotions also determine whether the altruistic emotions displayed are *proper* or *improper*, especially in relation to the scope, duration and intensity of these emotions. Rule-emotions such as feelings of guilt, justice and duty form, one could say, a *condition of justification* for the altruistic emotions.

It can be said that a person who has the disposition of a positive commitment to the well-being of his fellow man also has a positive attitude towards his *own* altruistic emotions. He identifies himself with these emotions and may even count it his duty to have these emotions; he can reproach himself – and worry – that he failed to have feelings of compassion or care for the other.

When a firm believer in Apartheid forgets his nationalistic, perfect duties for a moment and supports a black man who has been shot and takes him to safety, we will not call him a caring or friendly person if he later despises himself for his helpfulness. The person who is only now and then prepared to help, or who only helps one certain category of fellow human beings, is not the bearer of 'natural' virtues either; his actions are strongly determined by moods and prejudices. Un-reliability, prejudice and strict partiality are vices, while feelings of lovelessness, indifference, distrust and contempt are immoral emotions. Although altruistic emotions are in any case, and even in the first instance, directed at the weal and woe of the fellow human beings one is closest to (one's family and friends), they are also, if they are corrected by the rule-emotions, always concerned with the well-being and distress of other human beings (and animals). It is not coincidental that in the parable the Good Samaritan's compassion is directed towards an unknown man, probably from Judea, who is in trouble (Luke, 10: 25–37).

Rule-emotions, in particular the sense of justice, can counter (the danger of) the limited scope of the altruistic emotions. When this *limited* sympathy (Warnock) is not forced open, the danger threatens that people will only love passionately, and be loyal to, their own country, their own race or family and will, with great fanaticism, cold-bloodedness and indifference, humiliate and kill strangers and outsiders. Caring fathers and loving husbands have had their share in the massacres and genocides of this century. And when the love of one's own country and people leads to fanaticism, it becomes possible for the four hijackers of the ship *Achille Lauro* to execute 69-year-old Leon Klinghoffer, who had been confined to a wheelchair for years (*Time*, 21 October 1985). The distinction that B. Williams draws between the psychopath and the amoralist is of importance in this context. The crimes of the psychopath appal us because this human being is not capable of showing any feeling of sympathy or compassion whatsoever. The amoralist, however, does show some affection and does occasionally care for others. The mafia hitman, as we know him from the movies, does care for his dog, his mother, his child and his mistress. This gangster is still recognizably amoral, because he is extremely short on fairness and other general considerations:

> ... this man is capable of thinking in terms of others' interests, and his failure to be a moral agent lies (partly) in the fact that he is only intermittently and capriciously disposed to do so. But there is no bottomless gulf between his state and the basic dispositions of morality (Williams, 1972: 25).

To have altruistic emotions with respect to special persons is a necessary, but certainly not a sufficient condition for being a moral agent. The tentative conclusion can be drawn that the moral person has in any case acquired both types of moral emotions and their corresponding 'natural' and 'artificial' virtues.[6]

In concluding this part I will briefly explore the development of the capacity to *justify* moral rule-emotions. In order to have rule-emotions a person must have acquired a disposition of positive concern for moral rules and principles. A child will first acquire the moral rules, conventions and codes, and then – if the right pedagogical conditions are realized and the child has the necessary cognitive capacities – it will acquire the moral principles. With the help of these more abstract principles a moral person can justify or criticize the operative moral rules (Peters, 1974). This means that, in the development of the child, the motives and reasons for having rule-emotions will change. The manner in which a child perceives moral rules is to a high degree dependent on its cognitive development; Kohlberg's theory of the stages of moral development can offer us insight into this point. The justification which a child gives for its rule-emotions will vary according to the level of moral judgements which the child has attained – pre-conventional, conventional, or post-conventional. In any case, three forms of guilt can be distinguished: authority guilt, association guilt and principle guilt (Rawls, 1972: 467). 'Association guilt', for example, presupposes that the person is acquainted with the standards or rules which are fitting for the roles and duties of the individual in different social contexts such as family and school, and that she has thus acquired the cognitive capabilities needed to look at matters from different perspectives. Not only does the nature or justification of a certain rule-emotion change, the 'same' emotions – for example, 'guilt' from fear of losing a parent's love – can at a later stage no longer be called 'moral' (but 'neurotic').

5 The controversy between Kohlberg and Gilligan

Because of the fact that both types of moral emotions

presuppose and influence each other, important light can be shed on the controversy between Kohlberg and Gilligan.[7] Gilligan, as we know, criticizes Kohlberg's theory of moral development, because the experiences and concerns of women are insufficiently reflected in this theory. Kohlberg's conception of adulthood is out of balance, favouring the separateness of the individual self over its connection to others. On the basis of the responses of pregnant women to structured interview questions regarding the moral dilemma of whether to continue or abort a pregnancy, Gilligan concludes that the sequence of a woman's moral development follows a three-level progression from an initial focus on the self through a societal perspective, the discovery of the concept of responsibility as the basis for a new equilibrium between self and other, to a universal perspective. At this third level, both individual needs and conventions are subsumed under the moral principle of non-violence (Gilligan, 1977:483, 492). Gilligan stresses the centrality of the concepts of responsibility and care in a woman's construction of the moral domain, and she indicates that there is a close connection in women's thinking between concepts of the self and conceptions of morality (1977:516). According to Gilligan (1977), there are two distinct moral domains and moral languages, the domain of care and responsibility and the domain of justice and rights. The morality of responsibility which women describe stands apart from the morality of rights which underlies Kohlberg's theory (1977:509). The first domain is more typical for women and corresponds to the experience of the self as part of relationships, as 'connected self'; moral judgements, on the other hand, follow impartial rules defining rights and duties (cf. Lyons, 1983).

In his reply, Kohlberg admits that the 'principle' of altruism, care and responsible love has not been adequately represented in his works (Kohlberg et al., 1983:20). But he denies – and I think rightly so – that there are two different moral orientations. A morality of care and a morality of justice is a distinction made in the minds of all human beings, be they male or female (a belief also held by Gilligan in 1983). The growth of justice and the ethics of care do not represent two distinct tracks in the stages of moral development (Kohlberg *et al.*, 1983 : 139). According to Kohlberg, many moral dilemmas do not pose a choice between one orientation or another, but almost always call out a response which integrates the two orientations; in the Heinz dilemma the concerns for justice and care are often very hard to distinguish.

At first glance Kohlberg's conclusions seem to correspond to what I have asserted in relation to the two types of moral emotions. It is important, however, to stress the fact that Kohlberg is still interested only in the development of moral *judgements*:

> ... we partially accept Gilligan's differentiation of two orientations in moral *judgment* which may vary in stress from person to person and from situation to situation (Kohlberg *et al.*, 1983 : 138; my italics).

Gilligan's emphasis on the orientation of care and responsibility has (only), according to Kohlberg, broadened the moral domain beyond his initial focus on justice reasoning (Kohlberg *et al.*, 1983: 139). Care and responsibility, and also altruistic emotions such as compassion and concern, are thus subsumed under the category of moral judgement or reasoning. Gilligan, however, can be reproached for the same thing, though to a lesser degree. She repeatedly speaks, in connection with care, love and responsibility, in terms of a different 'mode of moral *judgment*', of a different 'way of thinking about conflict and choice' (1983: 49, 55, 58; my italics). Gilligan does not sufficiently recognize the specific nature of altruistic emotions, and it could be said that, in her research, she understands implicitly and describes this subclass of moral emotions as rule-emotions. But it is quite possible, as I have argued, that an explicit cognitive evaluation is omitted precisely in those cases where our altruistic emotions directly motivate us to act morally.

In Kohlberg's view, special obligations and relationships of care presuppose but go beyond the general duties of justice, which are necessary but not sufficient for them. Considerations of a special relationship – to one's own family and friends – are supererogatory, go *beyond* the duties owed to another on the basis of a person's rights (Kohlberg *et al.*, 1983 : 20–21). Many parents who take care of and protect their children do not however – always – feel themselves placed in a moral dilemma. They – often – act directly from feelings of love and care and not – constantly – from considerations of the rights of their child. Parents and caretakers do not – always – do more than they know they are obliged to, and are thus neither moral heroes nor saints. Most of the time they are motivated 'simply' by moral altruistic emotions.

Notes

1 R.S. Peters criticizes Kohlberg's theory of moral development for the fact that his system does not deal with the *affective* aspects of development (Peters, 1981 : 171). And G. Warnock states in his reply to R.M. Hare that

> ignorance is not a linguistic failing, nor is crass insensitivity, nor callous indifference. It is not through the study of language that these things are to be – as far as they ever will be – cured (Warnock, 1979 : 14).

2 I refer to the publications of W.P. Alston (1967), E. Bedford (1967), A.I. Melden (1969), G. Pitcher (1975) and J. Wilson (1971).
3 In his criticism of the ethics of Kant, Schopenhauer stressed the point that only those actions which are motivated by the weal and woe of others can be called truly 'moral'. Only in one case are actions not *egoistic* in nature:

> ... nämlich wenn der letzte Beweggrund zu einer Handlung, oder Unterlassung, geradezu und ausschliesslich im *Wohl und Wehe* irgend einer dabei passive betheiligten *Andern* leigt, also der aktive Theil bei seinem Handeln, oder Unterlassen, ganz allein das Wohl und Wehe eines *Andern* im Auge hat und durchaus nichts bezweckt, als dass jener Andere unverletzt bliebe, oder gar Hülfe, Beistand und Erleichterung erhalte. *Dieser Zweck allein* drückt einer Handlung, oder Unterlassung, den Stämpel des *moralischen Werthes* auf; ... (...) (...) es ist das alltägliche Phänomen des

Mitleids, d.h. der ganz unmittelbaren, von allen ander-
weitigen Rücksichten unabhängigen *Theilnahme* zunächst
am Leiden eines Andern und dadurch an der Verhinderung
oder Aufhebung dieses Leidens,...Dieses Mitleid ganz
allein ist die wirkliche Basis aller *freien* Gerechtigkeit und
aller *ächten* Menschenliebe (1840: 105, 106).

4 According to Zajonc preferences, or what he also calls 'affective
reactions' or 'affective judgments' [sic], need not depend on
cognition; we are therefore often unable to verbalize the reasons
for our attitudes or preferences. In my opinion, however, these
preferences do depend on *concepts* ('nice', 'attractive'), and also on
cognition, but not necessarily on a deliberate cognitive *evaluation*.

5 According to R.S. Peters the concern for others develops much
earlier in a child's life and does not require the same level of
conceptual development to be operative as does justice or even
honesty. It can be learned and encouraged by the example of
others. Of course, this concern for others can be exhibited at
different levels which vary according to a person's imagination
and sophistication about what constitutes human welfare.

But it certainly can get a foothold in a person's moral life
earlier than justice, because it is not necessarily connected
with rules and social arrangements, as is justice. This was one
of the reasons which led Hume to distinguish the artificial
from the natural virtues (Peters, 1974: 313).

6 J.L. Mackie states that, though *self-referential* altruism is a natural
virtue, it remains true that what we morally approve of and regard
as virtues in this area involve a wider concern for others than
either instinctive affection or immediate social intercourse would
produce. Humanity, generosity, compassion, clemency and
fairness must therefore be counted as *partly* artificial virtues with
respect to their approved range of application (Mackie, 1980: 127).

7 See also the publications of L. Kohlberg *et al.* (1983), N. Plessner
Lyons (1983), B. Puka (1983), *Ethics*, **92**, April 1982 (special issue
on 'Virtue, Sex and Gender: Some Philosophical Reflections on
the Moral Philosophy Debate'; contributions of O.J. Flanagan,
B. Puka, L. Kohlberg and others), G. Nunner-Winkler (1984).

References

Alston, W.P. (1967). Emotion and feeling. *In* P. Edwards (ed.), *The Encyclopedia of Philosophy*, Vol. 2, pp. 479-86. New York/London.

Arman-Jones, C. (1985). Prescription, Explication and the Social Construction of Emotion. *Journal for the Theory of Social Behavior*, **15**, 1-21.

Bedford, E. (1967). Emotions. *In* D.F. Gustafson (ed.), *Essays in Philosophical Psychology*, pp. 77-98. London/Melbourne.

Blum, L.A. (1980). *Friendship, Altruism and Morality*. London.

Boyd, D. (1983). Careful Justice or Just Caring: A Response to Gilligan. *Philosophy of Education: 1982. Proceedings PES*, 63-70. Normal, Ill.

Bridgeman, D.L. (ed.) (1983). *The Nature of Prosocial Development. Interdisciplinary Theories and Strategies*. New York.

Cochrane, D.B., Hamm C.M. and Kazepides, A.C. (eds) (1979). *The Domain of Moral Education*. New York.

Dent, N.J.H. (1984). *The Moral Psychology of the Virtues*. Cambridge.

Ethics (1982). Special issue on moral development, **92**.

Gilligan, C. (1977). In a Different Voice: Woman's Conceptions of Self and of Morality. *Harvard Educational Review*, 7, 481-517.

Gilligan, C. (1983). New Maps of Development: New Visions of Education. *Philosophy of Education: 1982. Proceedings PES*, 47-63. Normal, Ill.

Hare, R.M. (1979). Language and Moral Education. *In* D.B. Cochrane, C.M. Hamm and A.C. Kazepides (eds), *The Domain of Moral Education*. New York.

Hoffman, M.L. (1983). Affective and Cognitive Processes in Moral Internalization. *In* E.T. Higgens, D.W. Ruble and W.W. Hartup (eds) *Social Cognition and Social Development*, Cambridge.

Hoffman, M.L. (1984a). Interaction of Affect and Cognition in Empathy. *In* C. Izard, J. Kagan and R.B. Zajonc (eds), *Emotions, Cognition and Behavior*. Cambridge.

Hoffman, M.L. (1984b). Empathy, its Limitations, and its Role in a Comprehensive Moral Theory. *In* W.M. Kurtiness and J.L. Gewirtz (eds), *Mortality, Moral Behavior, and Moral Development*. New York.

Izard, C., Kagan, J. and Zajonc, R.B. (eds) (1984). *Emotions, Cognition and Behavior*. Cambridge.

Ben Spiecker

Kant, I. (1978). *Grondslagen van de ethiek. Grondslag voor de metafysica van de zeden.* Meppel.

Kohlberg, L., Levine, Ch. and Hewer, A. (1983). *Moral Stages: A Current Formulation and a Response to Critics.* Basel, London and New York.

Krebs, D. (1978). A Cognitive-developmental Approach to Altruism. *In* L. Wispé (ed.), *Altruism, Sympathy, and Helping. Psychological and Sociological Concepts.* New York.

Kurtiness, W.M. and Gewirtz, J.L. (eds) (1984). *Morality, Moral Behavior, and Moral Development.* New York.

Lyons, N.P. (1983). Two Perspectives: On Self, Relationships, and Morality. *Harvard Education Review,* 53, 125–45.

MacIntyre, A. (1967). Egoism and Altruism. *In* P. Edwards (ed.), *The Encyclopedia of Philosophy,* 463–6, New York.

Mackie, J.L. (1980). *Hume's Moral Theory.* London, Boston and Henly.

Melden, A.I. (1969). The Conceptual Dimension of Emotions. *In* Th. Mischel (ed.), *Human Action, Conceptual and Empirical Issues,* pp. 199–221. London.

Mussen, P. and Eisenberg-Berg, N. (1977). *The Roots of Caring, Sharing and Helping.* San Francisco.

Neblett, W. (1981). *The Role of Feelings in Morals.* University Press of America, Inc.

Nunner-Winkler, G. (1984). Two Moralities? A Critical Discussion of an Ethic of Care and Responsibility Versus an Ethic of Rights and Justice. *In* W.M. Kurtiness and J.L. Gewirtz (eds), *Morality, Moral Behavior, and Moral Development.* New York.

Peters, R.S. (1974). *Psychology and Ethical Development.* London.

Peters, R.S. (1981). *Moral Development and Moral Education.* London.

Pitcher, G. (1975). Emotion. *In* R.F. Dearden, P.H. Hirst and R.S. Peters (eds), *Reason. Part 2 of Education and the Development of Reason,* pp. 218–39. London and Boston.

Puka, B. (1983). Altruism and Moral Development. *In* D.L. Bridgeman (ed.), *The Nature of Prosocial Development. Interdisciplinary Theories and Strategies.* New York.

Rawls, J. (1972). *A Theory of Justice.* Oxford.

Richards, D.A.J. (1971). *A Theory of Reasons for Action.* Oxford.

Rorty, A.O. (ed.) (1980). *Explaining Emotions.* Berkeley.

Schopenhauer, A. (1840). *Preisschrift über das Fundament der Moral.* (Reprinted 1979, Hrsg. von H. Ebeling, Hamburg.)

Sichel, B.A. (1985). Woman's Moral Development in Search of Philosophical Assumptions. *Journal of Moral Education,* **14,** 149–61.

Spiecker, B. (1984). The Pedagogical Relationship. *Oxford Review of Education,* 10 (2).

Steutel, J.W. (1986). Education, Motives and Virtues. *Journal of Moral Education,* **15,** 179–88.

Warnock, G.J. (1979). Morality and Language: A Reply to R.M. Hare. *In* D.B. Cochrane, C.M. Hamm and A.C. Kazepides (eds), *The Domain of Moral Education.* New York.

White, J. (1984). The Education of the Emotions. *Journal of Philosophy of Education,* **18,** 233–44.

Williams, B. (1972). *Morality.* London.

Williams, B. (1973). Morality and the Emotions. *In* B. Williams (ed.), *Problems of the Self,* pp. 207–99, Cambridge.

Wilson, J. (1971). *Education in Religion and the Emotions.* London.

Wispé, L. (ed.) (1978). *Altruism, Sympathy, and Helping. Psychological and Sociological Concepts.* New York.

Zajonc, R.B. (1980). Feeling and Thinking. Preferences need no Interferences. *American Psychologist,* **35,** 151–75.

On seeking less than the best

MICHAEL SLOTE

It is usually assumed by philosophers and economists that practical rationality is subject to a condition of maximization: that the rational egoist, or the average non-egoist under conditions where the welfare of others is not at issue, will seek to maximize his own good, or well-being. Both utilitarians like Sidgwick and anti-utilitarians like Rawls seem to assume that it is egoistically, individualistically, irrational not to maximize one's satisfactions and seek one's own greatest good. More recently, however, some explicitly non-maximizing conceptions of personal well-being over time have been suggested by Amartya Sen and Charles Fried. But even in their non-maximizing conceptions of human good and the rational planning of lives, there is no suggestion that the egoistic individual should ever do anything but seek what is *best* for himself.

However, I shall be arguing here for just this sort of possibility. A number of conceptual and other objections naturally arise in connection with this thesis, and I shall first attempt to answer these objections and show that there is a space on our moral–psychological map for a non-optimizing form of egoistic rationality. Such non-optimizing rationality can exemplify one kind – perhaps the most important kind – of individual moderation, and I shall go on to argue that such moderation is not only not irrational, but is also an admirable tendency, a form of virtue.

The idea that a rational individual might seek less than the best for himself was originally developed, I believe, in the literature of economics. The term 'satisficing' was coined for such behaviour, and I shall make use of the term here. What the economists have done, however, is point to an aspect of human behaviour that philosophers have traditionally ignored, and I shall be discussing and articulating the idea of satisficing from the perspective of an attempt to give an adequate philosophical account of this phenomenon.

Consider an example borrowed from the economics literature. An individual planning to move to a new location and having to sell his house may seek, not to maximize his profit on the house, not to get the best price for it he is likely to receive within some appropriate time period, but simply to obtain what he takes to be a good or satisfactory price. What he deems satisfactory may depend, among other things, on what he paid for the house, what houses cost in the place where he is relocating, and on what houses like his normally sell at. But given some notion of what would be a good or satisfactory price to sell at, he may fix the price of his house at that point, rather than attempting, by setting it somewhat higher, to do better than that or do the best he can. His reason for not setting the price higher will not, in that case, be some sort of anxiety about not being able to sell the house at all or some feeling that trying to do better would likely not be worth the effort of figuring out how to get a better price. Nor is he so rich that any extra money he received for the house would be practically meaningless in terms of marginal utility. Rather he is a 'satisficer' content with good enough and does not seek to maximize (optimize) his expectations. His desires, his needs, are moderate, and he may not be particularly interested in doing better for himself than he is likely to do by selling at a merely satisfactory price. If someone pointed out that it would be better for him to get more money, he would reply, not by disagreeing, but by pointing out that for him at least a good enough price is good enough. Such a person apparently fails to exemplify the maximizing and optimizing model of individual rationality traditionally advocated by philosophers. But I think he none the less represents a possible idea of (one kind of) individual rationality.

Here is another example. Imagine that it is mid-afternoon: you had a good lunch, and you are not now hungry; neither, on the other hand, are you sated. You would enjoy a candy bar or Coca Cola, if you had one, and there is in fact, right next to your desk, a refrigerator stocked with such snacks and provided gratis by the company for which you work. Realizing all this, do you then, necessarily take and consume a snack? If you do not, is that necessarily because you are afraid to spoil your dinner, because you are on a diet or because you are too busy? I think not. You may simply not feel the need for any such snack. You turn down a good thing, a sure enjoyment, because you are perfectly satisfied as you are. Most of us are often in situations of this sort, and many of us would often do the same thing. We are not boundless optimizers or maximizers, but are sometimes (more) modest in our desires and needs. But such modesty, such moderation, need not be irrational or unreasonable on our part.

Of course, moderation has been exalted as a prime virtue in many religious and philosophical traditions. But when, for example, the Epicureans emphasized the rationality of moderation in the pursuit of pleasure, they recommended modesty in one's desires only as a means to an overall more pleasurable, or less unpleasant, life, and in the example mentioned above moderation is not functioning as a means to greater overall satisfactions. One is not worried about ruining one's figure or spoiling one's dinner, and the moderation exemplified is thus quite different from the instrumental virtue recommended by the Epicureans. The sort of moderation I am talking about, then, is not for the sake of anything else.

But then isn't the moderate individual who is content with less a kind of ascetic? Not necessarily. An ascetic is someone who, within certain limits, *minimizes* his enjoyments or satisfactions; he deliberately leaves himself with less, unsatisfied. The moderate individual, on the other hand, is someone content with (what he considers) a reasonable amount of satisfaction; he wants to be satisfied and, up to a certain point, he wants more enjoyments rather than fewer, to be better off rather than worse off; but there is a point beyond which he has no desire, and even refuses, to go.

Now the kind of example just mentioned differs from examples of satisficing mentioned in the literature of economics. Economists who have advocated the model of rational satisficing for individuals, firms or state bodies have pointed out that, quite independently of the costs of gaining further information or effecting new policies, an entrepreneur or firm may simply seek a satisfactory return of investment, a satisfactory share of the market, a satisfactory level of sales, rather than attempting to maximize or optimize under any of these headings. But writers on satisficing generally seem to hold that satisficing only makes sense as a habit of not seeking what is better or best, rather than as a habit of actually rejecting the better, when it is clearly available, for the good enough.

However, the example of the afternoon snack challenges this limitation. For the individual in question turns down an immediately available satisfaction, something he knows he will enjoy. He is not merely not trying for a maximum of enjoyments, but is explicitly rejecting such a maximum. And I think that most of us would argue that there is nothing irrational here.

At this point, however, it may be objected that the example may be one of rational behaviour but is less than clear as an example of satisficing. The individual in question prefers not to have a certain enjoyment and certainly deliberately rejects the maximization of his pleasures. But it is not clear that the moderate individual must think of himself as missing out on anything *good* when he forgoes the afternoon snack. For although he knows he would enjoy the snack, the very fact that he rejects such enjoyment might easily be taken as evidence that he does not in the circumstances regard such enjoyment as a good thing.

In order to deal with our doubts, it may be useful at this point to consider other examples, more purely hypothetical than the present one, where the good forgone through satisficing is fairly obvious.

How do we react to fairy tales in which the hero or heroine, offered a single wish, asks for a pot of gold, for a million dollars, or, simply for (enough money to enable) his family and himself to be comfortably well off for the rest of their lives. In each case the person asks for less than he might have asked for, but we are not typically struck by the thought that he was irrational to ask for less than he could have.

The individual in the fairy tale who wishes for *less* than he could, presumably exemplifies the sort of moderation discussed earlier. He may think that a pot of gold or enough money to live comfortably is all he needs to be satisfied, that anything more is of no particular importance to him. At the same time, however, he may realize (be willing to admit) that he could do better for himself by asking for more. He need not imagine himself constitutionally incapable of benefiting from additional money or gold, for the idea that one will be happy or satisfied with a certain level of existence by no means precludes the thought (though it perhaps precludes *dwelling* on the thought) that one will not be as well-off as one could be. It merely precludes the sense of wanting or needing more for oneself. Indeed, the very fact that someone could actually explicitly wish for enough money to be comfortably well-off, is itself sufficient evidence of what I am saying. Someone who makes such a wish clearly acknowledges the possibility of being better off and yet chooses a lesser but personally satisfying degree of well-being. And it is precisely because the stakes are so large in such cases of wishing that they provide clearcut examples of presumably rational individual satisficing.

But at this point some doubt may remain about our description of the moderate individual's response to being granted a wish. He may make the seemingly modest wish he does because he is afraid of offending the wish grantor or in order to avoid corrupted (or rendered blasé) by having too much wealth, and thus motivated, he will not exemplify the sort of satisficing moderation whose non-irrationality I have tried to defend: he *will* be seeking what is best for himself under a refined conception of personal good that goes beyond mere wealth or material comfort.

With this I can absolutely agree. An individual who asks for less than he could may indeed be motivated by factors of the above sort. My main point is, and has been, that there is no reason to insist or assume that such factors are always present when an individual asks for less than that he can obtain. From the standpoint of the phenomenology of our own lives, it does not seem as if such factors are always present. Why insist that some other factor(s) must always be present to turn putative cases of satisficing into cases, fundamentally, of optimization or maximization of the individual's (perceived) good?

The situation here resembles what is often said for and against psychological egoism. Nowadays, philosophers at least seem to recognize that altruism and self-sacrifice cannot be ruled out *a priori*. None the less, it in some sense remains empirically open that human altruism may turn out to be an illusion. It is conceivable, let us suppose, that a powerful enough psychological theory that entailed the universal selfishness of human behaviour might eventually be adopted. But in the absence of such a theory, philosophers have been, I think, quite right to insist upon taking altruistic motivation seriously.

And similar points can, I believe, be made about satisficing or moderation in the sense delineated earlier. Perhaps, it will someday be definitively shown by economists and/or psychologists that the best explanation of why humans act as they do requires us to assume that they are always maximizing or optimizing and thus that apparent examples of satisficing or moderation are illusory. But until and unless that happens, we should recognize – something philosophers have not previously noticed or admitted – that the common-sense understanding of our own lives leaves a definite recognizable place for occasional, perhaps even frequent, satisficing moderation. Moreover, it is a mere confusion to say (as I have heard it said) that the person who turns down a certain good is none the less inevitably seeking his own good in some more refined sense, because the person is maximizing the satisfaction of his preferences on the whole, among which, after all, is presumably the preference not to have that unnecessary good (and/or the general preference not to have much more than he needs). The same form of argument would be laughed out of court if applied in the area of morality and altruism: we all know by now that it would be absurd to argue that the individual who sacrifices his life for others must be seeking his own greatest good in doing so, because in doing so he is maximizing his weighted preferences, one very powerful one of which is the preference that he should die so that others should live.

However, it is also possible, while not denying the existence of moderation, to hold that the rejection of the better for the good enough is, when it occurs, irrational. In response to my account of satisficing moderation, for example, Philip Pettit has argued that the person who rejects what is better for himself in favour of what he considers good enough may have a reason for choosing what he chooses – what he chooses is, after all, good enough – but has no reason to choose what he chooses in preference to what he rejects. There may be reason to wish for or choose moderate wealth or well-being, but there is no reason for the moderate individual I have described to choose moderate wealth over great wealth, and for that reason, according to Pettit, his choice counts as irrational or unreasonable.

This objection, however, is extremely problematic. It is not, to begin with, a general condition of rationality that in choosing between two options one has (a) reason to choose one of those options rather than the other. When two equally good or self-beneficial options present themselves, it need not be irrational to choose one of them, even though one has no reason to prefer it to the other. In the second place, reasons can be relative to individuals' concerns, their world view, or even their habits; and from the distinctive standpoint of the moderate individual, there may well be a reason to prefer moderate wealth (well-being) to great wealth (well-being). The fact that great wealth is much more than one needs (or cares about) can count, for such an individual, as a reason for rejecting great wealth and choosing moderate wealth, but of course such a reason will not motivate, or even occur to, someone who always seeks to optimize. The moderate individual will thus sometimes have a reason to prefer what is less good for herself, but a reason precisely of a kind to lack appeal to the maximizing temperament.

I would like now to focus on the question of whether there is anything particularly praiseworthy about satisficing moderation. I think, however, that we shall be in a position to make a proper evaluation of moderation only if we put the opposing tendency towards optimizing into proper perspective. It has sometimes been pointed out that the optimizing tendency may be in some measure self-defeating. A person bent on eking out the most good he can in any given situation will take pains and suffer anxieties that a more casual individual will avoid, and it is hardly clear that the pains and anxieties will (on average) be compensated for by goods garnered through optimizing alertness and energy. But this point hinges on psychological contingencies, and in fact the habit of optimizing also has intrinsic, essential features in the light of which I think we shall inevitably think less well of those who have that habit.

Consider first, how much more planful and self-conscious the continual optimizer must be in comparison with the satisficer who does not always aim for the best and who sometimes rejects the best or better for the good enough. The satisficer need not consider and compare as many possibilities as the optimizer – indeed, quite typically, the satisficer will pursue the first option he notices; if it seems reasonably satisfactory, he will not bother even to consider other possibilities. The habit of optimizing essentially has an unspontaneous and constrained aspect, and we to some extent feel sorry for, think less well of, someone lacking in spontaneity and constrained in his behaviour.

The optimizing person is possessed of other negative features that further serve to undercut our antecedent sense that optimizing rationality is a desirable or admirable human trait. The optimizing individual – again, as a matter of conceptual necessity, not of accidental psychology – seems lacking in self-sufficiency. We value and admire self-sufficiency in the ordinary sense of the term (which is not the extreme notion used by the Stoics), and a sober ideal of self-sufficiency can in fact be used as a touchstone for the criticism of optimization. Consider, again, how the optimizer appears to others. Will not his tendency to eke out the most or best he can in every situation strike someone who witnesses or hears about it as lacking in self-sufficiency? Will not the optimizer appear needy and grasping and his persistent efforts a form, practically, of desperation, by contrast with the satisficer who accepts the good enough when he gets it? So I am saying, among other things, that there is an inherent connection between aiming for what one takes to be sufficient, rather than for what is best, and a kind of personal self-sufficiency that most of us think well of. The habit of optimization must, therefore, be taken as an anti-virtue, an unfortunate and lamentable human character trait. And the habit of moderation then naturally takes its place as a desirable trait, a virtue.

Our previous discussion has tended toward the conclusion that we should think less well of the (purely) optimizing temperament than of the disposition towards satisficing moderation. However, in comparing satisficing and optimizing to the detriment of the latter, I have not yet said anything specifically against the *rationality* of optimizing.

Let me do so now. Both altruism and moderation are traits requiring cultivation within the individual. In some sense they do not come naturally, and parents, teachers, and others have a difficult task on their hands when they attempt to overcome or mitigate children's insatiable selfishness and greed. The typical simplified picture of how a child develops intrinsic concern for others involves the assumption that children need to go through an intermediate stage where they see a concern for others as furthering their own interests, and a similarly simplified picture of the attenuation of childhood demandingness and greediness might well depict the child as having to go through a stage where moderation was seen (in the Epicurean manner) merely as a means to greater overall satisfaction (the cake will spoil your dinner or give you a tummy ache). But just as the development of some degree of intrinsic concern for others is typically regarded as a form of moral progress, I believe that the development of some degree of non-instrumental moderation is also a good thing, a kind of human progress.

By contrast, an unwillingness to do anything but optimize would commonly be regarded not only as unattractive but as irrational. Most of us think there are entirely satisfactory levels of well-being or well-doing less than the best one can conceive or hope for, and someone who cannot be content with some such level, someone who persists in looking and trying for something better even when he has attained such a level, seems to us compulsive, insatiable and certainly irrational (even apart from the relative costs and benefits of the efforts involved). But this does not mean that we think only moderate individuals are practically rational. Some people want more than they merely need; even when they see they are fine and well off as they are, they may prefer to do better than that. But such people are not necessarily insatiable, and it is only the insatiable at the one extreme and the ascetic (or masochistic) at the other, who from a common-sense standpoint represent *clear* cases of irrationality.

The implications of this analysis for educational psychology and educational practice may be of some interest. Would it not be worthwhile to do empirical studies of the development of moderation in individuals along the lines of recent studies of moral development? Should we not be interested in instilling certain values of practical rationality into school children if we are already committed to thinking that schools should educate for moral values; and will it not then be important to ascertain, again empirically, how rational values, like moderation, are best taught or inculcated? Questions like these are rather neglected in recent educational experiment and theory; but if satisficing is as central to reasonable living as my earlier discussion would suggest, they are probably well worth pursuing.

73

Bibliography

Rawls, J. (1971). *A Theory of Justice*. Cambridge, Massachusetts.

Sen, A. (1979). Utilitarianism and Welfarism. *Journal of Philosophy*, 76, 463-89.

Sidgwick, H. (1962). *The Methods of Ethics*. London.

Simon, H. (1955). A Behavioral Model of Rational Choice. *Quarterly Journal of Economics*, 69, 99-118.

Slote, M. (1983). *Goods and Virtues*. Oxford.

Slote, M. (1985). *Common-sense Morality and Consequentialism*. London.

Competence as an aim
of education

WOLFGANG BREZINKA

Competence (in German: *Tüchtigkeit*) is an ideal of personality
with a long history. In ancient Greece it was known as *aretè*. In
ancient Rome it was called *virtus*. In Germany since 1919 it has
been included as an aim of education in several constitutional
laws. In the Youth Welfare Law (Gesetz für Jugendwohlfahrt)
it appears as follows: 'Every German child has a right to
education with the aim of physical, mental, and social
competence' ('Jedes deutsche Kind hat ein Recht auf
Erziehung zur leiblichen, seelischen und gesellschaftlichen
Tüchtigkeit' – *Jugendrecht*, 1985: 11).

Competence is one of the world's oldest educational aims,
but it is no longer self-evident. Because of its general nature it
has become vulnerable to the suspicion of representing merely
an 'empty prescription'. It appears problematic to some people
because it tends to suggest ideas of requirements, achievement,
competition, and compulsion to conform.

Can we still use competence as an educational aim? What can
it contribute to ideological and moral orientation? What are its
implications for the theory of moral education? What would
change if we were to give it up?

In order to answer these questions we must first know the
meaning of the word 'competence'. To this end I will begin by

referring to a few characteristics of a more precise concept of competence. Then I will treat the anthropological convictions underlying the ideal of competence. Finally, I will evaluate this educational aim.

1 The concept of competence

'Competence' means a relatively permanent quality of personality, which is valued positively by the community to which the person belongs. It is the ability of an individual to meet specific demands which are placed upon him to their full extent. This ability is acquired as the result of personal effort.

The quality of competence is attributed to a person who shows himself *to be up to those tasks* which *life presents to him*. 'To be competent' means *to be able to do what is required*. Competence is always related to something which must be completed, performed or achieved. Such demands and tasks either grow out of specific situations, or they are placed on the person by some external agent, or the person imposes them on himself.

Competence is always connected to requirements. There is no competence without a specification as to the area in which somebody is or should become competent. We can speak of competence meaningfully only in connection with requirements. But requirements do not exist in general, they are always *specific* requirements. Competence is always related to specific requirements and its content is determined by them. For this reason it is impossible to attribute to a person competence as such, without reference to particular tasks or kinds of tasks.

A person is competent by being able to perform a certain kind of task. If a person possesses the disposition for certain kinds of achievement then he is described as competent in relation to this task: 'competent to work', 'professionally competent', 'a competent sportsman', 'morally competent', and so forth. There are as many kinds of competence as there are requirements and corresponding dispositions.

It is essential to the concept of competence that this disposition is acquired as the result of *individual effort*. Competence is not an inborn quality. It does not develop by itself, neither through maturation nor solely by incidental learning; rather, it requires intentional learning. Every form of competence is within the power of the individual and its acquisition is voluntary (Aristotle, 1956). It is a quality acquired by action in the form of repeated exercise. It is unattainable without specific intention, readiness for effort, and expedient action. Only through persistent effort can an individual learn to carry out an activity so well that it deserves the name of competence.

In every sphere of human activity competence is the result of practice: with verbal, manual, scientific, sporting, or musical ability as well as with moral virtues. In every case, as Aristotle writes,

> it is by similar activities that habits are developed in men; and in view of this, the activities in which men are engaged should be of (the right) quality, for the kinds of habits which develop follow the corresponding differences in those activities. So in acquiring a habit it makes no small difference whether we are acting in one way or in the contrary way right from our early youth; it makes a great difference, or rather all the difference (1975: 22).

The individual is thus just as responsible for the 'merits of his character' as for the 'forms of his inferiority'. For better or for worse we are 'co-producers of our basic attitudes' by either repeated similar actions or repeated similar omissions (Aristotle, 1956: 57).

Finally, a remark concerning the characteristic: 'requirements must be met *to their full extent*'. This means the same as satisfying them *well*. This excludes qualities which are '*just sufficient*', which lie just above the border of inability. On the other hand, it leaves the concept of competence applicable to all degrees up to outstanding quality.

The standard that is to be used in each case is the specific requirement. It does not have to be the same for all the members of a group, but rather can be reset for people who are handicapped in order to take the limits of their ability into account as well. Competence can thus be defined according to the degree of achievement which can reasonably be expected from each individual.

I will conclude these remarks with the following definition: competence is a relatively permanent personal quality to satisfy certain requirements to their full extent. It is acquired through individual effort and is positively valued by the community.

2 Anthropological foundations of the ideal of competence

In order to evaluate what the ideal of competence can contribute to ideological and moral orientation, we must consider the anthropological foundations it is based upon. Only if these assumptions are empirically well founded does it make sense to expect some help from this ideal for education. There are three main assumptions.

2.1 Every human being by nature depends on being formed by society and culture as well as by himself

Man is born with a mental constitution which is open, plastic and determinable by experience. He is extremely capable of learning and in need of learning. Nature does not provide him with his personality as a finished product; rather, the personality forms itself gradually as a result of its own actions and experiences in life. Between birth and the end of adolescence he is forced to acquire a certain state of personality which enables him to live his life well according to the specific conditions of his society and its culture. His character and to a certain degree even his body are under a 'compulsion to learn' or a 'compulsion to be formed' (cf. Brezinka, 1971, 1981a, b; Gehlen, 1950: 63). Once he has achieved adulthood he is not only a 'work of nature' but also a 'work of society' and a 'work of his own doing' (Pestalozzi, 1946: 192). Expressed differ-

78

ently: 'One becomes good and virtuous through three things, namely predisposition, habit, and insight' (Aristotle, 1973: 239).

There is no comprehensive name for the influencing factors which must supplement the inborn qualities of his organism before an individual becomes competent for life (*lebenstüchtig*). Since Plato and Aristotle, however, three kinds of influences have been emphasized as being of special importance: first, the pressure (or 'compulsion') emerging involuntarily from his fellow men and the surrounding order of culture (or the 'laws'); secondly, education; and thirdly, conscious self-determination through practice and insight. Kant distinguished between 'external compulsion' and 'free self-compulsion' (1982: 508, 509, 512).

Another name for this culturally dependent condition of competence is 'discipline'. According to Kant 'the culture of discipline' is necessary for the 'creation of a reasoning being's competence in all its forms'. It 'consists of the liberation of the will from the despotism of the desires' (1981: 390).

Arnold Gehlen has emphasized even to the point of one-sidedness that character is a 'product of discipline' which results from the acts of its owner and from the effects of the actions of others upon him. He describes man as 'a being to be disciplined'. In man 'the physis is of such a quality that it is necessarily also a *task*. This means that we cannot think of human nature without thinking of qualities like discipline, control, responsibility, and values'. 'That man is a task for himself' extends even 'to the responsibility for the quality of his physis' (Gehlen, 1950: 365, 373, 401).

This idea that man is not only a 'co-producer' of his mental attitudes but, to a certain degree, of his physical assets and defects as well, was already familiar to Aristotle. He who leads a life without discipline becomes sick; he who neglects physical training becomes ugly. Also with regard to the physical appearance 'repeated specific acts', or their repeated neglect, bring about 'a corresponding state of personality' (Aristotle, 1956: 55).

How this cultivation of one's own personality by action and

79

omission is achieved was described by Nietzsche as follows:

> Our actions form us: in every action certain forces are trained and others not, and thus temporarily neglected. One emotion always re-enforces itself at the expense of other emotions whose power it saps. The actions which we carry out most frequently finally incase us: they claim our powers, thus making the execution of other intentions more difficult. – In the same way a person is formed by regular omissions: whether he has exerted self-control or self-indulgence a few times every day will become obvious. – This is the primary consequence of every action: it adds something to us, – of course also physically (Nietzsche, 1978: 240, 241).

This view of human nature and of the becoming of personality is *opposed* to those ideas which fall under the concepts of *nativism* and *evolutionsim*. These concepts are used here to designate the theory that the personality 'develops' or 'evolves' from inborn predispositions in which its qualities are already present. One thinks of this evolution taking place according to the pattern of the maturation of physical organs, a process which follows an inherited plan and which is only slightly under the influence of experience. This view is not borne out by facts and has already been refuted many times. There is overwhelming evidence that the personality results out of learning, actions, exercises, experiences, ideas and decisions.

2.2 The habituation of behaviour in accordance with cultural norms is a prerequisite for coping with life

The term 'habituation' is used here for the learning process by which repeated experiences and/or actions of the same type give rise to a habit, that is, a relatively permanent mental disposition for a certain type of behaviour. The phrase 'in accordance with cultural norms' means a type of behaviour which conforms to socio-cultural norms and is for this reason valued positively by the community. These norms are not limited to moral and legal norms, but they also include language norms, hygienic, economic, technical, scholarly, aesthetic, religious, professional, athletic, and other norms. On the side of the adult members of the community certain forms of knowledge, convictions, and abilities correspond to these norms, enabling them to act according to them. These different 'convictions', 'attitudes', 'skills' and 'virtues' can be summarized under the concept of the *'good habit'* (Willmann, 1908: 97; Mausbach, 1920: 84).

Only by habituation of behaviour in accordance with cultural norms can the plastic constitution of a newborn child gradually be transformed into a competent personality. The sum of the qualities acquired by habituation has been called since antiquity 'the *second nature*' of man. Due to his natural plasticity, openness and ability to learn, man 'depends on a second nature . . . in order to be able to live with his first nature' (Hofstätter, 1958: 117). In other words, man must master his ways of thinking and doing to such a degree that they are carried out smoothly and without conscious thought, as if they were 'natural' processes emerging of 'their own accord'.

Examples of this include the mastery of one's mother tongue, all kinds of social abilities and working skills. The mastery of knowledge is of the same kind: habituated knowledge 'is knowledge which can be put to use instantly in every concrete practical situation, knowledge which has become "second nature" and which can be adapted to the task at hand, to the demand of the moment' (Scheler 1954: 36). This is equally true of attitudes and convictions: they 'guide the course of our experience with great precision in such a way that one can almost speak of a "reflexive" control of thought'. 'This automatism constitutes the enormous biological importance of attitudes: in problem situations they present themselves to consciousness immediately, as decisions which have already been finished in a way that places them beyond all doubt, thus eliminating the need for the machinery of decision-making to be activated; they make possible the solution of problems which would otherwise have to be submitted to time-consuming consideration if the attitude did not exist.' For this reason attitudes and convictions are 'first-rate tools for managing problematic situations'. They are the 'stabilizers of personality', 'labour efficiency aids', 'sources of security' (Rohracher, 1976: 394).

Valuable habits are of course only necessary but not sufficient conditions for successfully coping with life. Another misunderstanding must also be avoided. When emphasizing the indispensability of habituated ideas and actions we do not mean to play down the importance of intellectual alertness, the critical use of reason, and adaptability to new situations. On the contrary: both, the role of reason as the most important human power, and of prudence as the most important virtue (indeed, the basis of all other virtues), are essential to the adherents of the ideal of competence. It is not reason that is played down here, but *intellectualism* (or rationalism), i.e. the unrealistic overvaluation of thinking as the *only* means of controlling the personality.

2.3 The acquisition and maintenance of moral competence are dependent upon a relatively lasting social order

Upon his entry into the world every individual finds a particular social order with a particular way of life. Law, morals and custom are its most important components. Allegiance to the demands they make is expected of all members of the group. The inclination to believe in valid norms and to orient oneself according to them is acquired through early familiarization with their demands. If children and adolescents are to identify themselves with these norms it is necessary that the grown-ups believe in and habitually act according to them. This is only possible when the group's social order is relatively permanent and when its members adhere to it without reservation.

This relation has already been emphasized by Aristotle: moral competence depends on a moral order of society which 'has the power to assert itself'. 'In the polis', according to Aristotle, its power is provided by 'law and custom' (1956: 238–9). But law and custom can bring about the acquisition and maintenance of virtue only if they are relatively durable:

'The law can only assert itself through the force of habit, and this emerges only with time, so that easy transition from existing laws to different new ones leads ultimately to the weakening of the power of law' (Aristotle, 1973: 89).

In this view, every individual is regarded as part of a trans-individual social system, in *contrast* to *individualism* and *moral subjectivism*. Moral convictions and moral competence are not the products of inborn autonomous impulses. Instead, they arise in reaction to the moral demands and social pressures of the family and the community.

The moral order of society is established before the individual appears, and each member is influenced by it to the very core of his mind. His inner stability depends to a large degree on the support from the outside moral order (Brezinka, 1981b: 62).

This view implies a belief in the indispensability of *authority* and *tradition*, in order to ensure the self-preservation of communities and the moral competence of their members. This does not exclude an acute awareness of the dangers of the abuse of authority and the petrification of tradition. Strongly tradition-bound communities carry within themselves the threat of 'the stultification which is always lurking shadow-like behind stability' (Nietzsche, 1976: 583). On the other hand, 'a society in which revolt against tradition becomes universal . . . damns itself to extinction' (Kolakowski, 1978: 378).

3 The evaluation of competence as an aim of education

How is competence as an aim of education to be evaluated? What can it offer for ideological and moral orientation? How does it emerge in comparison with competing educational aims? Should we give it up or hold on to it?

I will begin with the arguments in favour of 'competence' as an educational aim. Then I will describe two competing educational aims often mentioned nowadays and show their shortcomings. Based on these arguments I will finally make a recommendation.

3.1 Advantages of competence as an aim of education

Let us recall once again the most important characteristics of the concept of competence. 'Competence' is used here to mean the ability of an individual to meet specific demands to their full extent. Competence presupposes that each individual is faced with certain tasks or requirements whose fulfilment is valued positively by the community. Competence can be acquired only by personal effort. Competence can be increased to the level of perfection. It is, however, also possible for handicapped persons to be competent if they meet the demands appropriate to them. What is the value of competence as an aim of education?

(a) The educational aim of competence is very general, but can be further delimited

The concept of competence is small in content and wide in application. It can be applied flexibly because it is the common denominator of a wide range of personality traits. On the other hand, it can be further delimited by additional characteristics. This is attained by filling the indeterminate (or formal) concept of 'certain requirements' with information regarding the type of requirement actually involved. The educational aim of competence becomes more concrete (or more determinate) the more concrete the requirements to be met.

Competence as such, without greater specification of its content, exists only as an abstract concept. In reality competence occurs always in a specific form. The general concept of competence has, however, the advantage that it can express everything common to all concrete forms of competence, thus facilitating overview and mutual under-standing. It is neutral with regard to all social systems and can thus be used by any group to designate group-specific ideals of personality by adding further specifications (cf. Meister, 1965: 19).

But also as a general concept, 'competence' contributes to a realistic interpretation of human nature regardless of specific ideological, moral and political convictions. It serves as a reminder that every person is faced with tasks and must strive for perfection in order to become and remain competent. *What* these tasks are can be concretized by every possible specification of the general concept of competence.

(b) The ideal of competence stresses the importance of socio-cultural demands in the life of man, but is also compatible with their historical relativity

Competence presupposes that men are dependent upon communities and their culture which make demands that must be met as well as possible. It is an ideal which considers man as bound to communities, dependent upon cultural norms, and obligated to fulfil communal tasks. It helps to counterbalance the dangers of unbridled egotism.

In addition to that this ideal is compatible with the relativity of cultures. It does not have the same absolute content for all people, but is instead adaptable to the specific conditions of every community, in particular to its economy, its political order, its religion, its ideology, and its morality present at a given time. The ideal of competence can be related equally to requirements faced by entire groups as well as those confronting individual persons.

(c) It emphasizes the personal activity and responsibility of the educand

Competence is a quality which must be 'acquired through personal effort', 'through zeal and diligence', as Cicero writes (cf. Willmann, 1908: 98). Wherever competence is an ideal, it is understood that it stems only from personal activity and that it is honourable to strive for it.

This goes hand in hand with the conviction that every person is responsible for his own actions and omissions and thus for their effects upon his own character. In good and evil he is not only a 'work of nature' and a 'work of society', but also a 'work of his own doing' (Pestalozzi, 1946). He is not merely a product of chance but he can and must determine himself, albeit within certain limits.

(d) It favours the striving for perfection

The essential characteristic of competence is 'the ability to meet specific demands to their full extent'. 'To their full extent' is a standard that does not allow for minimal performances. But it does allow higher degrees of performance up to excellence. It is an ideal that links social approval as well as self-esteem to good performance.

This sets a high level of aspiration which also influences the ideal self-image. A person who recognizes the ideal of competence demands much from himself and becomes dissatisfied with himself when he fails. Because every kind of ability can be intensified to the level of perfection, the ideal of competence opens wide-ranging goals and thus many possibilities for gratifying activities, happiness with success, and the experience of meaning. It is an ideal which favours an active life. It opposes the overestimation of pleasure and places more value on work as the precondition of a happy life. It fits to that image of man characterized by Goethe at the end of *Faust*: 'Whoever puts himself to strain, he will find salvation.' For Goethe, 'competent' ('tüchtig') was one of his favourite moral concepts (cf. Korff, 1955: 665; Boucke, 1901: 9).

3.2 Competing aims of education and their deficiencies

The educational aim of competence is no longer approved by all groups of society. Some reject it expressively, others have simply allowed it to be forgotten. It is often difficult to find out whether merely the *word* 'competence' is being devalued, or whether the *ideal of personality* represented by the word has lost its credibility.

In the first case, where the *word* is the subject of devaluation, the ideal is retained while the old name for it is neglected or abandoned. This might be so because the word seems worn out or because of negative associations. In such cases a new, unblemished name is attached to the old concept. The same was true for a time of the word 'virtue': the word was avoided but the concept was retained and expressed with less problematic words such as 'moral attitude' or 'moral competence'. This phenomenon seems to be repeating itself in the case of the German word *Tüchtigkeit*: the ideal remains valid but some people prefer to label it with other words, for instance 'competence' or 'qualification'. The second case is more problematic: here it is not just a matter of the renaming of the same ideal. Instead, completely different ideals with other characteristics and other anthropological foundations are set up which stand in opposition to the ideal of competence. An educational aim which poses an *absolute* contradiction to competence, i.e. one which excludes *all* the characteristics of our concept, is extremely hard to conceive of. The differences are usually less significant than they seem. They are based partially on misunderstandings created by the ambiguity of the common meaning of 'competence' and by unfamiliarity with the explicated concept.

What at first glance appears to be strict rejection frequently turns out to be something quite different when submitted to semantic analysis, namely a relative devaluation of certain types of competence in favour of other personal qualities which, upon closer examination, also fall under the concept of competence. Only through such analysis can we determine whether concepts proposed as substitutes for competence are really new (that is, a combination of characteristics which have nothing in common with competence) or whether there has simply been a change of names.

Thus we must examine more closely the question of whether those educational aims apparently competing with the aim of competence actually compete with it. As a rule this will only be the case when the educational aim under discussion is based on a different anthropological view than the ideal of competence. As we have seen, there exist above all three conceptions irreconcilable with this ideal: (1) nativistic and evolutionistic theories of personality, (2) intellectualism and (3) individualism and moral subjectivism.

The fundamental difference between the use of a different name with the same meaning and the choice of a completely different concept must be considered carefully if we want to interpret correctly the indications of a decline in interest in competence as an aim of education.

Which educational aims are recommended as substitutes for the aim of competence or, more precisely, for the different kinds of competence? I will discuss here only those two which are propagated most widely at the moment: (a) the freely developed personality; and (b) the 'ability of moral judgment' at the highest level (cf. Kohlberg and Turiel, 1971: 442).

(a) The freely developed personality

All over the world it has been suggested that the 'free development of the personality' should be laid down as the most general aim of education. This trend is based on the UN Declaration of Human Rights and on the human rights articles in national constitutions. In the Federal Republic of Germany, Article 2, Paragraph 1 of the constitution (*Grundgesetz*) is relevant:

> Everyone has the right to *the free development of his personality* to the extent that he does not infringe upon the rights of others and does not violate the constitutional order or the moral law (cf. Peters, 1953).

The purpose of this human right is, however, completely different from the purposes of educational aims: this right serves to protect citizens from arbitrary intervention by the state in their personal lives.

The 'free development of the personality' is a fundamental human right. But if it is declared as an aim of education it becomes an empty formula without any normative content. Fundamental rights guarantee freedoms; among them the freedom to educate and to be educated. But fundamental rights are not aims of education. One can take the 'free development of the personality' as an educational aim only if one has no clear idea of what an educational aim actually is and what purpose it serves.

An aim of education is a norm describing a particular mental disposition (or a network of dispositions) set as an ideal for an educand. The same norm requires the educator to act in a way that enables the educand to realize this ideal to the greatest degree possible. The most important purpose of educational aims is to give educators orientation for educational action. At the same time they serve as standards for the evaluation of educational success (Brezinka, 1981a: 150).

We can speak of an aim of education only if a specific quality of personality is described as an ideal, i.e. as something that should be. That 'development of the personality' does not qualify as an educational aim is confirmed by the failure of the word 'development' to designate a specific quality of personality. Instead this word designates a process eventually resulting in a 'fully developed' or relatively complete personality. The naming of such a process contributes absolutely nothing to the definition of an educational aim. It is not part of the definition of educational aims, but can in this context only cause confusion.

We can try to avoid such confusion by interpreting the phrase 'free development of the personality' as having the following meaning: 'the personality which has developed freely' or 'the freely developed personality'. This is the interpretation I have chosen. It is the only possible interpretation, if we take seriously the claim that an aim of education is meant. Instead of the process of 'development' this formula emphasizes the 'personality' and its qualities.

But this detour does not lead anywhere, because the characteristic 'freely developed' is not a quality of personality or a disposition. It only expresses something about the circumstances which are believed to contribute to the coming into being of personality: independent, uncommitted, without being influenced by external agents, the result of the unhindered development of inherited predispositions. This obviously never occurs in reality. But even were this the case, the reference to the *development* of the personality provides no information at all about the *state* of the personality which is recommended as an ideal. Process-oriented concepts such as 'development' are completely unsuited for the designation of educational aims, which requires product- or disposition-oriented concepts (cf. Brezinka, 1981a: 52, 112). Thus the phrase 'freely developed personality' is without any prescriptive content.

Untenable aims like this can only be propagated if the differences between a state of personality and the conditions for its realization, or between a desired product and the conditions of its production, are not understood. Instead of naming the only important characteristics of educational aims – the desired qualities of personality (or mental dispositions) – the concept of free development emphasizes something which has nothing to do with an aim: a vague nativist–evolutionistic idea of the making of personality connected with equally vague notions of the educator's duty to respect the 'freedom' of the educand. Obviously there is no reason to object to this duty or to the educand's freedom – as long as they are interpreted realistically – but they do not belong to normative statements on aims of education. Instead they concern educational actions as a means for the realization of educational aims.

The false belief in the 'freely developed personality' as an aim of education has been encouraged above all by Article 26, Paragraph 2 of the United Nations' General Declaration on Human Rights of 10 December 1948: 'Education shall be directed to the full development of the human personality...' In Article 29 again, the 'free and full development of his personality' is mentioned (Joyce, 1978: 12).

When we examine the context of these rather questionable formulations it becomes clear that their primary function is to protect the rights and freedoms of citizens from inadmissible state interference, while simultaneously stating the limits formed by the 'rights and freedoms of others' as well as the 'just requirements of morality, public order and the general welfare' (Article 19, Paragraph 2). The justified interests of the individual are being considered here in addition to those of society, but this in no way alters the fact that the 'free and full development of the human personality' cannot serve as an aim of education. For this reason, it cannot serve as a substitute for the educational aim of competence.

(b) The ability of moral judgement at its highest level
This is an educational aim which has been presented as a substitute for moral competence. It has been advocated

primarily by the American psychologist Lawrence Kohlberg whose work is based on John Dewey and Jean Piaget. It has found many adherents in a short time. Its basis is provided by a complicated theory of so-called 'moral development' whose validity remains controversial (cf. Schreiner, 1979, 1983).

For our present discussion, it is important that Kohlberg has established his theory expressly in opposition to the aims and methods of 'traditional moral education', which he considers 'indoctrinating', 'undemocratic', and 'unconstitutional'. He sees its aims in 'cultivating a bag of virtues', that is 'a set of approved traits such as honesty, responsibility, friendliness, service' and so forth (Kohlberg and Turiel, 1971: 412, 413, 421). Kohlberg considers virtues to be questionable educational aims in public schools, because in modern pluralistic societies there is a lack of consensus over these 'moral character traits generally considered to be positive'. At best there is the appearance of consensus: concepts of virtue or moral character are essentially vague and 'noncontroversial' only for this reason. According to Kohlberg 'it is *impossible to define the content of moral education* in terms of factual majority consensus about good and bad behavior' (1971: 420, 424). He thus prefers us to limit ourselves to the *formal* aim of the ability to make 'mature moral judgments'.

Kohlberg starts from the assumption that there exist six stages of moral development. For him the most important differences are judgement according to societal 'conventions' on the one hand (stages 3 and 4), and judgement according to 'standards which have been critically examined and agreed upon by the whole society' (stage 5), as well as 'universal principles of justice, of the reciprocity and equality of the human rights, and of respect for the dignity of human beings as individual persons' on the other hand (stage 6). Instead of aiming at virtues of 'fixed virtues' in order to reach 'conformity to society's code', education should be directed to the ability to make 'post-conventional' or 'autonomous' moral judgements according to principles (Kohlberg and Turiel, 1971: 413, 415, 428).

This is not the place for a critical examination of Kohlberg's moral–pedagogical views as a whole. My purpose is to question whether his condemnation of virtues as educational aims is well-founded and whether the aims recommended by him as substitutes are actually superior to the virtues.

The answer to both questions is 'no'. Kohlberg is apparently not familiar with the classical concept of virtue. What he calls 'virtue' and 'bag of virtues' is a self-created phantom stemming from ignorance in philosophy, from unrealistic criticism of culture and from perfectionistic prejudices. He characterizes his ideological standpoint as 'progressivism' and 'ethical liberalism' (Kohlberg and Mayer, 1972: 454, 472). The opposite is seen by him in those anthropological views which hold the transmission of culture to be the main purpose of education. Such views are 'society-centered' and emphasize, according to him, 'the common and the established'. Their educational aims are defined in 'trait words' related 'to a conventional cultural standard which is...ethically relative'. Educational aims merely represent not more than 'particular community conventions' and are thus 'arbitrary' (1972: 454, 478, 479).

Kohlberg insinuates that 'the cultural transmission model views the development of the mind through the metaphor of the machine'. He supposes it to be based upon a primitive psychological stimulus-response theory traceable from John Locke to Edward Thorndike and B.F. Skinner.

Kohlberg has so little idea of the Aristotelian–Thomistic origins of the concept of virtue and of its anthropological foundations that a single objection may suffice here. It is certainly true that adherents of behaviourism have supported the transmission of culture as the task of education, but it is absurd to identify support for virtues and cultural trans-mission with support for behaviourism, which Kohlberg, incidentally, caricatures in the most primitive way as 'mechanistic'. In no place does he provide conclusive evidence for a rejection of virtues as aims of education. On the contrary, Kohlberg himself cannot manage without the concept of virtue – only he does not seem to have realized that his own educational aims also fall under the concept of virtue.

As evidence, let us look at the aims which he recommends as substitutes for virtues. I will not treat here the view of 'development as the aim of education' because I have already refuted it. Leaving this so-called aim aside the following aims remain: the ability for 'mature moral judgement', also known as 'enlightened' morality. This is described as 'the structural capacity for principled reasoning'. It 'means understanding and acceptance of the principles of justice and human welfare which are the foundations of our constitutional democratic society'. This ability is abbreviated as 'a sense of justice': 'Educationally, the aim of stimulating mature moral reasoning is the development of a sense of justice' (Kohlberg and Turiel, 1971: 461, 464).

Although Kohlberg considers trait words to be 'unnecessary', 'superfluous' and 'misleading', he in fact uses them himself when naming his educational aims (Kohlberg and Mayer, 1972: 478). For without doubt such words as 'attitude', 'competence', 'ability', 'morality', 'sense of justice', and 'just' or 'free character' are expressions which designate mental dispositions (cf. Brandt, 1970). The classical name for such dispositions towards morally valuable action is, however, 'virtue'. Kohlberg's 'ability for moral reasoning on the highest level' is conceptually nothing else but an essential element of the old virtue of prudence. Kohlberg's 'sense of justice' is an essential component of the virtue of justice (cf. Pieper, 1940, 1953).

Why is it necessary to emphasize that Kohlberg considers only *parts* of virtues? Because anthropologically he is an adherent of *intellectualism*. He refers expressively to the teaching of Socrates that virtue consists in *knowledge* of the good: 'He who knows the good chooses the good'; 'the reaching of virtue is the asking of questions . . ., not the giving of answers' (Kohlberg, 1980: 26). This view has already been criticized by Aristotle, who pointed out that knowledge of the good as such does not enable man to do the good. Virtue does not stem only from insights but above all from action, exercise and habituation. In contrast to Socrates and Plato, Aristotle teaches that 'without such action, no one has the slightest prospect of ever becoming a morally valuable person' (1956: 33).

Kohlberg overestimates the intellectual bases of moral action and ignores its habitual and emotional (or motivational) bases. The concept of moral education is much too wide for the narrow area to which Kohlberg limits himself theoretically and practically. He is interested only in *instruction*, which is supposed to stimulate *thinking* about moral *problems*. He concentrates exclusively on the ability of moral *judgement*. However, virtue is the ability of moral action – understood as the readiness, inclination, habit or disposition leading to morally good action. This is the reason why Kohlberg's educational aims cannot serve as a substitute for the aims of moral competence or virtue.

One cause of Kohlberg's contradictions and lack of clarity is his confusion of ends and means, and of educational aims and the methods for their realization. In this he is like his predecessors Dewey and Piaget. His polemic against virtues and 'bags of virtues' as educational aims is generally not what he thinks it is, but rather a critique of certain *methods* of moral education that is partly justified (Kohlberg and Turiel, 1971: 412).

In order to be fair, it must be mentioned that Kohlberg more recently revised his ideas about moral education substantially. Parallel to the change in public opinion from the radical cultural–revolutionary ideas of the American academic protest movement to neo-conservatism, Kohlberg came to recognize the importance of that which he earlier denounced as mere 'conventions' and 'indoctrination'. He admitted that his theoretical assumptions about the sixth and highest stage of 'moral development' had not been confirmed by empirical research. None of his test subjects could be said to have reached the sixth stage, not even in adulthood. On the existence of sixth-stage-persons he later wrote: 'Maybe it was all my imagination' (1980: 27). At any rate, Kohlberg came to recognize the morality of the 'conventional level' as the most important aim of education, and the methods he later recommended are no longer merely 'Socratic': 'Our approach is not merely Socratic..., it comes close to the indoctrinative.' His aim was no longer 'attainment of the fifth stage but a solid attainment of the fourth-stage commitment of being a good member of a community or a good citizen' (1980: 28). While his adherents among the radical critics of Western society still propagate him as an 'avant-gardist' and 'the chief witness of critical-emancipatory educational programs' who has 'developed programs for strengthening the ability to make moral judgments without reference to traditionally set moral standards' (Regenbogen, 1984: 8), Kohlberg himself returned to the 'conventional' virtues as aims of education which he formerly opposed so violently.

3.3 A final recommendation to accept competence and virtues as aims of education

The comparison of the ideal of competence with two other general aims of education widely recommended today brings me to a final decision in favour of competence. There is no reason to give up the ideal of competence as an aim of education. On the contrary: it is more important for modern society than ever. Why?

First of all, because the requirements which must be met under the complicated conditions of our culture have become more numerous and demanding. Secondly, because individual dependence on the abilities, performance and virtues of known and unknown fellow men has increased radically due to the heightened division of labour and specialization of tasks. Thirdly, because a society greatly differentiated by cultural, political and ideological pluralism needs shared basic ideals which ensure a common order of life and which protect against the forces of dissolution (cf. Brezinka, 1986: 28). The ideal of competence – if defined specifically according to the particular order of life – can serve this purpose better than any other ideal.

Even in its most *general* form it gives orientation. It helps to ensure that abilities, knowledge and virtues are recognized as the most important and valuable personality traits. It directs attention to the tasks and requirements which are considered important within the community. It furthers the willingness to make efforts and the striving for self-perfection. These are aids of decisive importance for offsetting the risks inherent in the egalitarian welfare state: hedonism, privatism, moral minimalism. By this I mean the temptation to offer minimal performance while making maximal claims; the parasitic tendency to live at the expense of others; exclusive concentration on the pursuit of personal pleasure; the inability to limit voluntarily one's own desires; the aversion to social integration and subordination (cf. Bell, 1976; Kelpanides, 1985).

In order to avoid these dangers, common ideals are needed to raise those basic attitudes on which the real welfare of the individual and the common weal depend. They have to be *specific* ideals appropriate to the nature of man as a being in need of discipline, and appropriate to the conditions of modern life. As far as I can see these ideals of personality and aims of education can be defined sufficiently well only by using the concepts of competence and virtue. For this reason I recommend that we restore them to their rightful place in educational theory. In so doing we would be continuing a great European tradition.

References

Aristotle (1956). *Nikomachische Ethik*. Werke, Vol. 6. Translated by F. Dirlmeier. Darmstadt.
Aristotle (1973). *Politik*. Translated and Edited by O. Gigon. München.
Aristotle (1975). *The Nicomachean Ethics*. Translated with Commentaries and Glossary by H.G. Apostle. Dordrecht and Boston.
Bell, D. (1976). *The Cultural Contradictions of Capitalism*. New York.
Boucke, E.A. (1901). *Wort und Bedeutung in Goethes Sprache*. Berlin. Reprint Leipzig 1977.
Brandt, R.B. (1970). Traits of Character: A Conceptual Analysis. *American Philosophical Quarterly*, 7, 23-37.
Brezinka, W. (1971). *Erziehung als Lebenshilfe. Eine Einführung in die pädagogische Situation*. Wien.

Brezinka, W. (1981a). *Grundbegriffe der Erziehungswissenschaft.* München.

Brezinka, W. (1981b). *Erziehungsziele, Erziehungsmittel, Erziehungserfolg. Beiträge zu einem System der Erziehungswissenschaft.* München.

Brezinka, W. (1986). *Erziehung in einer wertunsicheren Gesellschaft. Beiträge zur Praktischen Pädagogik.* München.

Gehlen, A. (1950). *Der Mensch. Seine Natur und seine Stellung in der Welt.* Bonn.

Hofstätter, P.R. (1958). Die Sozialanpassung und die zweite Natur des Menschen. *Jahrbuch für Psychologie und Psychotherapie,* 6, 112–19.

Joyce, J.A. (ed.) (1978). *Human Rights. International Documents.* Alphen.

Jugendrecht (1985). München.

Kant, I. (1981). *Kritik der Urteilskraft.* Werke, W. Weischedel (ed.), Vol. X. Frankfurt.

Kant, I. (1982). *Die Metaphysik der Sitten.* Werke, W. Weischedel (ed.), Vol. VIII. Frankfurt.

Kelpanides, M. (1985). Zur Problematik der normativen Integration in wohlfahrtsstaatlich organisierten Demokratien. *Zeitschrift für erziehungs- und sozialwissenschaftliche Forschung,* 2, 189–226.

Kohlberg, L. (1980). High School Democracy and Educating for a Just Society. *In* R.L. Mosher (ed.), *Moral Education. A First Generation of Research and Development,* pp. 20–57. New York.

Kohlberg, L. and Mayer, R. (1972). Development as the Aim of Education. *Harvard Educational Review,* 42, 449–96.

Kohlberg, L. and Turiel, E. (1971). Moral Development and Moral Education. *In* G.S. Lesser (ed.), *Psychology and Educational Practice,* pp. 410–65. Glenview, Ill. and London.

Kolakowski, L. (1978). Der Anspruch auf die selbstverschuldete Unmündigkeit. *In* W. Oelmüller, R. Dölle and R. Piepmeier (eds), *Diskurs: Sittliche Lebensformen,* pp. 378–89. Paderborn.

Korff, H.A. (1955). *Geist der Goethezeit,* Vol. IV. Leipzig.

Mausbach, J. (1920). *Grundlage und Ausbildung des Charakters nach dem hl. Thomas von Aquin.* Freiburg.

Meister, R. (1965). *Beiträge zur Theorie der Erziehung.* Neue Folge. Graz.

Nietzsche, F. (1976). *Werke.* K. Schlechta (ed.), Frankfurt.

Nietzsche, F. (1978). *Die Unschuld der Werdens. Der Nachlass,* Vol. II. Stuttgart.

Pestalozzi, J.H. (1946). Meine Nachforschungen über den Gang der Natur in der Entwicklung des Menschengeschlechts. *In* E. Bosshart *et al.* (eds), *Gesammelte Werke*, Vol. 8. Zürich.

Peters, H. (1953). Die freie Entfaltung der Persönlichkeit als Verfassungsziel. *In* D.S. Constantopoulos (ed.), *Gegenwartsprobleme des internationalen Rechts und der Rechtsphilosophie*, pp. 669–78. Festschrift für Rudolf Laun. Hamburg.

Pieper, J. (1940). *Traktat über die Klugheit*. Leipzig.

Pieper, J. (1953). *Ueber die Gerechtigkeit*. München.

Platon *Sämtliche Werke*, Vol. 1. Heidelberg, sine anno.

Regenbogen, A. (ed.) (1984). *Moral und Politik – soziales Bewusstsein als Lernprozess*. Köln.

Rohracher, H. (1976). *Einführung in die Psychologie*. Wien.

Scheler, M. (1954). Die Formen des Wissens und die Bildung. *Philosophische Weltanschauung*, pp. 16–48. München.

Schreiner, G. (1979). Gerechtigkeit ohne Liebe, Autonomie ohne Solidarität? Versuch einer kritischen Würdigung der Entwicklungsund Erziehungstheorie von Lawrence Kohlberg. *Zeitschrift für Pädagogik,* **25,** 505–528.

Schreiner, G. (1983). Auf dem Weg zu immer gerechteren Konfliktlösungen. Neue Anmerkungen zur Kohlberg-Theorie. *In* G. Schreiner (ed.), *Moralische Entwicklung und Erziehung*, pp. 103–132. Braunschweig.

Willmann, O. (1908). *Philosophische Propädeutik. Part II: Empirische Psychologie*. Wien.

Learning the virtue of self-control

JAN STEUTEL

1 Is the virtue of self-control a pure ability?

Most members of the older generation disapprove of the uncontrolled behaviour of their children. They punish the undesirable impulsivity of their descendants and discourage their uninhibited expression of aggression. They reward their appropriate showing of patience and they encourage the required suppressing of their inclinations. In performing these activities they intend to stimulate the development of self-control.

Although many parents attach great value to the disposition[1] of self-control, it is not my intention to examine the (un)desirability of this educational aim. In this paper I would like to answer a question which (logically) precedes such a normative inquiry. A positive formulation of this question is: if the members of the grown-up generation stimulate the virtue of self-control, *what* then is it that they pursue? And the negative formulation of the same question is: if the members of the half-grown generation have not (yet) acquired the virtue of self-control, *what* then is it that they are missing?

1.1 Does the virtue of self-control include specific motives?

In the vast majority of more or less recent essays on virtue, a distinction is made between virtues and abilities. This distinction basically comes down to the following. In contrast with abilities, virtues include a certain *motivational* component, in the broad sense of the word. When we claim that someone is the bearer of certain virtues, we imply above all that such a person possesses dispositions to *choose*, to *want* or to *prefer* something, or that someone *takes care* of something or has become *committed* to something. G. Ryle thus warns us against an interpretation of virtues in terms of abilities, skills, competences or capacities (cf. Ryle, 1958, 1972). Virtues are rather certain 'educated tastes and cultivated preferences'. The honest man, for example, has learned 'to dislike deception'; and the charitable man has the 'want to relieve distress' (1958: 151). We find a similar view in a well-known essay on virtue by P. Foot (cf. 1978: 4–8). According to her, virtues, in contrast with such abilities as memory and concentration, are conceptually related to intentions, desires, wants and attachments: 'a virtue is not ... a mere capacity: it must actually engage the will' (p. 8). Even the virtue of (practical) wisdom involves certain tendencies, such as the pursuit of what is really worthwhile and important in human life (cf. pp. 6–7).

These examples can be supplemented without difficulty.[2] Essentially, they always come down to the same thing: when we credit a person with a certain virtue, we express our opinion on the nature of his *motives*: we say something about the content of his wants and aversions. However, when we credit someone with a certain ability, we only say that such a person *can do* something: we do not assert anything about his wants and aversions. Following in the footsteps of R.B. Brandt (1970), I will from now on call this conception the *motivation theory of virtues and vices*.

On first impression this explanation of virtues sounds credible. Numerous virtues can in fact be understood (at least partially) as specific motives, that is to say as wants and aversions with regard to certain behaviour or states of affairs.[3] For example, honesty implies an aversion toward deceit and toward illegally appropriating the property of others; conscientiousness involves the want to honour one's duties and an aversion toward shortcomings in one's devotion to duty; and benevolence contains the want to promote the well-being of one's fellow man and an aversion toward injuring the well-being of one's neighbour. And the same thing applies *mutatis mutandis* to other virtues.

But the fact that *many* virtues can (partially) be understood as specific motives says little about the validity of the motivation theory as such. For this theory implies that *all* virtues are interwoven with certain wants and aversions. And it is this implication that in my opinion is doubtful. If my view is correct, there is at least one virtue which cannot be confined to the motivational interpretation, namely the virtue of *self-control*.[4] This disposition, I suggest, does *not* include specific motivational components but is an ability *pur sang*. Or, to put it more correctly perhaps, to learn the virtue of self-control and to acquire a collection of abilities amount to the same thing.

1.2 Can lack of self-control be an expression of inability?

In the Department of Functional Psychology and Methodology at the Free University of Amsterdam, research is being done into problems of attention and behaviour of children at school. E. Das-Smaal has recently published some of the results of this study (1985; Das-Smaal *et al.*, 1987). Experienced teachers from normal elementary schools were asked to compare the behaviour of present-day pupils with that of the pupils of about ten years ago. The teachers agreed with each other in many respects: the present-day pupil is more restless, fidgety and impulsive; his ability to concentrate has decreased and he is even less able to concentrate over a longer period of time; and his perseverance is not what it used to be: he gives up sooner in case of a set-back.

Although the term 'self-control' does not appear in the

research report or in the questionnaire which was used, I think that it was this phenomenon which was really at stake. More than that, one could conclude from the results of the study that the teachers feel, among other things, that the present-day pupil shows little self-control, at least in comparison with his predecessor of about ten years ago. I will advance both an empirical and a conceptual argument in support of this interpretation.

The first argument is derived from an empirical study by W. Mischel and his colleagues (Mischel, 1974: 252–4; Mischel 1976: 155, 458–9). According to this psychologist the ability to refuse immediate gratification voluntarily, to tolerate self-imposed delays of reward, is one of the most important forms of self-control (cf. Mischel and Ebbesen, 1970: 329; Mischel and Mischel, 1977: 32–3). In order to determine the construct validity of 'self-imposed delay of gratification', Mischel examined the possible connections between this dimension of self-control and (other) cognitive, intellectual and personality variables. This study clearly confirmed that there are, among other things, significant relations between self-imposed delay of gratification and such variables as the degree of impulsivity and the capacity for sustained attention. In other words, what the teachers from the study by Das-Smaal were worried about, namely restless, impulsive behaviour and the underdeveloped ability to sustain one's attention for a considerable time, correlates to a large extent with a certain deficiency of an important dimension of self-control.

The second argument is a purely conceptual one. Das-Smaal's report states that the pupil of today has difficulty in awaiting his turn and gives up soon if something does not succeed straight away. In other words, according to the teachers consulted, the present-day pupil shows too little patience and too little perseverance. The dispositions of patience and perseverance are known as *instrumental virtues*, which also include diligence, constancy and temperance. One of the most important functions of instrumental virtues is to correct certain (counter-)inclinations. Patience, for example, forms a counterbalance to such motivating emotions as resentment and boredom; and perseverance has (among other things) the function of calling a halt to the inclination to abandon important goals in adversity (cf. Roberts, 1984a). So, to accuse someone of lacking in showing instrumental virtues (including patience and perseverance), is *ipso facto* to reproach that person for showing too little *control* of the corresponding (counter-)inclinations.

On the basis of these two arguments, let us assume that the study in question is also concerned with the degree of self-control pupils have. And let us assume further that the teachers' view is accurate. To what then could one attribute this apparent lack of practising self-control? Why is it that the present-day pupil shows less self-control in comparison with his predecessor?

If my objection to the motivation theory is correct, if the virtue of self-control should be understood as a pure ability, then a certain failure in practising self-control can depend on two factors.

In the first place it can depend on the degree of *motivation* to practise the disposition of self-control. Although crediting someone with an ability says nothing about the nature or presence of any motive whatsoever, *using* an ability is of course subject to the occurrence of wants and aversions. This is also true of the ability for self-control. Practising this disposition implies that motives occur even though the specific character of these wants and aversions is unlimited from a logical point of view. That is why it is quite possible for a person to be capable of controlling certain inclinations *without* being motivated to do so. The pupil can control himself, but he does not want to, at least not when the teacher wants it.

In the second place, insufficient practise of self-control can be blamed on a certain measure of *inability*. Although a person is sufficiently motivated to control his inclinations, he is not capable of doing so. The pupil wants to control himself, but he cannot, at least not when the teacher expects it.[5]

Of course, philosophical research cannot determine which variable plays the greatest role. That can only be done by doing empirical research. But I can, from a philosophical angle, clarify the specific nature of these two variables. And in view of the central question of this paper, I am especially interested in the second cause: if the pupil cannot control himself, what does he miss? If a lack of self-control is due to an inability what then is wrong with the pupil?

Until now I have brought forward two theses. In the first place, I have stated that the motivation theory of virtues and vices is not tenable: the virtue of self-control does not include specific wants and aversions. In the second place, I have asserted that a certain deficiency in practising self-control can logically be a manifestation of an inability. Both theses are based on the *same* idea: the virtue of self-control is a pure ability. Up to this moment I have only assumed this. It has now become time to defend this idea and to work it out. I will do that by first examining our concept of practising self-control (section 2), followed by a return to the theses mentioned (section 3).

2 Exercising self-control: a conceptual analysis

Everyday language has many phrases and expressions which refer to forms of self-control: 'to force oneself to do something', 'to resist temptation', 'to break bad habits', 'to fight boredom', 'to keep one's countenance', 'to suppress urges'. And my question is: on what grounds are the acts that are summed up here forms of self-control? Or, to formulate it in more general terms, to what does an act have to conform in order to be justifiably called an act of self-control? I shall answer this question by describing two necessary conditions. Together these complex conditions are sufficient for making the expression 'exercising self-control' applicable.

2.1 A first condition: conflicting motives

In the first place, a person performs acts of self-control *only if a conflict exists between his preference(s) on the one hand, and his occurrent (counter-)inclination(s) on the other*. I will first give an abstract explanation of this description; an illustration then follows with the help of two examples.

Preferences are wants which are connected to specific *cognitions*, namely the actor's belief that performing an action, or refraining from an action, is under the circumstances the best thing to accomplish. By that I do not mean that the person thinks the performance or forbearance is best *in a certain respect* (for example, in a moral, prudent, juridical or technical respect), but that he is of the opinion that performing the action, or abstaining from the action, is *all in all* or *all things considered* the most suitable thing to accomplish.[6] These cognitions accompany the occurrence of preferences.

Many of us know from our own experience that certain wants and aversions can make it difficult for us to realize our preferences. Such wants and aversions I will call *inclinations* and *counter-inclinations* respectively. These motives are passions, desires, impulses and activating feelings which come into conflict with our preferences in concrete situations. Inclinations urge us to perform actions which we all in all do *not* consider to be the best, while counter-inclinations threaten to stop us from carrying out actions which we *do* consider to be the best. And acts of self-control are performed only in situations in which we are touched by inclinations or counter-inclinations, that is to say in which occurrent wants and aversions conflict with our preferences.[7]

I shall make this abstract exposition more concrete by means of two examples. These examples belong to two important subclasses of self-control, which I shall call respectively cases of *restraint* and cases of *endurance*.

The first example concerns little John. He has decided to save his pocket-money with the intention of buying a beautiful bike at some later point of time. Long before he has saved enough, he walks past a toy store with his money in his pocket. When he sees all those inviting toys, his money starts to burn a hole in his pocket. Only with difficulty does he resist the temptation to go into the shop and spend his money immediately.

This standard example shows a conflict between a *preference* on the one hand and a want or *inclination* on the other. In order to buy a bike, John thinks that all in all the best thing to accomplish is not to spend his money; but at the same time he has an occurrent inclination to do so.

We can consider this example a case of *restraint*. These are instances of self-control in which the actor has (i) a preference to abstain from doing X; (ii) the inclination to perform X; and (iii) the expectation that performing X, or its short-term effects, will be pleasant, agreeable or enjoyable.

In the second example, little William is the principal character. He plans to clean up his room in order to surprise his mother. But this is much harder for him to do than he thought. William simply hates cleaning up. It is only with great difficulty that he manages to overcome his reluctance and tidy his room.

In this paradigmatic example a *preference* conflicts with an aversion or *counter-inclination*. With a view to pleasing his mother, William feels that all things considered the best thing to do is to clean up his room; but a counter-inclination nearly prevents him from doing so.

This example is one of *endurance*. In such cases the actor has (i) a preference to perform Y; (ii) a counter-inclination with regard to performing Y; and (iii) the expectation that performing Y, or its short-term effects, will be tiresome, unpleasant or disagreeable.[8]

2.2 *A second condition: self-intervention*

In the second place, a person performs acts of self-control *only if he intervenes in his want(s) and/or aversion(s) with the intention of accomplishing that which he prefers.* I shall first give a general comment on this description as well; after that a further clarification follows by way of some examples from developmental psychology.

Someone who controls himself is not passive but *active*. Such a person is not purely a spectator of the conflicts between his preferences and his (counter-)inclinations; he is not someone who waits to see which wants and aversions will win in the end and determine his behaviour. On the contrary, a person who exercises self-control *does* something. He *forces* himself to go to the dentist; he *withstands* the temptation to help himself; he *tempers* his feelings of resentment and spite; he *suppresses* his urge to steal. Behind these verbs numerous overt and covert activities lie hidden through which the actor influences his wants and aversions. For this reason, the philosopher W.P. Alston (1977: 76 ff.) calls such activities forms of *self-intervention*. The self-controller intervenes in his wants and aversions by doing things, for instance by weakening the causal strength of his inclinations or by supporting his preferences with powerful wants. And this is all done with the intention of realizing his preferences; for the person who exercises self-control has by definition the expectation that his preferences will be overruled *unless* he turns to self-intervention.

In developmental psychology, a great deal of empirical research has been done into the processes of self-intervention. Although the term 'self-intervention' is not used in the research reports, the subject is emphatically present. Mischel and his colleagues in particular have done fascinating studies in this field. The two clusters of examples of self-intervention which I shall discuss are taken from their research. These examples can also be understood as instances of two important subclasses of self-control, which I will call cases of *mitigation* and cases of *stimulation*.

The first cluster of examples concerns forms of self-intervention in *waiting*-situations. In a series of experiments, Mischel and his colleagues examined the psychological processes which make the delay of gratification either more difficult or easier. For this research project, pre-school children (between the ages of 4 and 5) were placed in a special room meant for experimental purposes. In this room they were shown two rewards by the experimenter – a small one (e.g. one marshmallow or one pretzel) and a larger one (e.g. two marshmallows or two pretzels). The children preferred the larger reward but could only earn this by waiting for the experimenter to return to the room of his own accord. They could obtain the smaller, unpreferred reward by breaking off the waiting on their own initiative, for instance by signalling the experimenter with a bell. And the question was: which psychological mechanisms influence the length of waiting for the preferred but delayed reward?

The first series of experiments (cf. Mischel and Ebbesen, 1970; Mischel *et al.*, 1972) confirmed that the average waiting time becomes shorter as the child keeps his attention fixed more pointedly on the rewards. On the other hand, the waiting period becomes longer if the child *distracts* his attention from the rewards by using certain *self-distraction techniques*. Some children stopped watching the rewards by putting their hands before their eyes or by putting their heads on their arms; other children began to talk to themselves, thought up games to play with their hands and feet, or started to sing ('This is such a pretty day, hurray'); still other children were told to look at irrelevant but comparable objects, or to think of pleasant things such as playing with attractive toys. By performing these activities, the children suppressed their attention for the rewards. And these covert and overt distracting responses considerably favour the delay of gratification.

Experiments carried out later (cf. Mischel and Moore, 1973, 1980; Mischel and Baker, 1975; Moore *et al.*, 1976; Moore, 1977) brought to light psychological mechanisms of a somewhat different kind. It was discovered not only that the length of the waiting period is influenced by whether or not attention is given to the marshmallows and pretzels, but equally by *the way in which* attention is given to the rewards. Like so many other stimuli, the rewards in question have certain consummatory or arousing qualities 'such as the pretzel's crunchy, salty taste or the chewy, sweet, soft taste of the marshmallows'. If a child notices these qualities the waiting period becomes very short indeed. The waiting time becomes considerably longer if the child practises certain *cognitive transformation techniques*. These techniques consist of transferring one's attention from the consummatory qualities to the non-consummatory or informating qualities, for example 'by thinking about the pretzel sticks ... as long, thin brown logs or by thinking about the marshmallows as white, puffy clouds or as round, white moons' (Mischel and Baker, 1975: 259). This transformational non-consummatory ideation makes delay of gratification considerably easier.

If we now interpret this first cluster of standard examples according to the previously developed terminology, the following reconstruction comes about. The children in the cited experiments have the same *preference*. They prefer earning the larger reward and, all in all, they think it is best to wait. But this preference conflicts with certain *(counter-) inclinations*. The children are teased by aversive frustration, connected with the want to call back the experimenter. The causal strength of these occurrent (counter-)inclinations becomes greater if the child pays attention to the rewards, particularly to their consummatory qualities.[9] In order to prevent these (counter-)inclinations from determining his behaviour, the child practises *self-intervention* (whether or not he is told to do so by the experiment leader). This intervention means carrying out the self-distraction techniques and the cognitive transformation techniques which were mentioned earlier. By using these techniques, the child distracts his attention from the consummatory qualities which act as frustrating stimuli. And the result of all this is that the strength of his (counter-)inclinations *diminishes*.

We can explain this group of examples as instances of *mitigation*. These are cases of self-control in which the actor (i) has a preference either to abstain from doing X or to perform Y; (ii) has the inclination to perform X or a counter-inclination with regard to performing Y; and (iii) intervenes with the intention of mitigating the causal strength of this (counter-) inclination.

A second cluster of examples concerns forms of self-intervention in *working*-situations. In contrast to a waiting-situation, achieving one's goal in a working-situation is dependent on the execution of certain tasks. In waiting-situations 'rewards are contingent only on the passage of time'; in working-situations 'rewards are contingent on the completion of work (Patterson and Carter, 1979: 272; cf. Mischel *et al.*, 1972: 216; Mischel, 1974: 273, 1981: 252).

As the above has shown, fixing one's attention on the

consummatory qualities of the rewards is an ineffective strategy – in waiting-situations anyway. But the reverse is true in working-situations. In that case cognitive attention for the rewards in fact makes the exercise of self-control *easier*. Experiments by Mischel and Patterson (1976), for instance, have confirmed this. They studied the performance of children in working-situations. The children in question could earn the more attractive reward (in this case, playing with 'fun toys') if they accomplished a certain task (placing a peg into every hole on a pegboard) within a set time. While executing this task the children were constantly being distracted by 'Mr Clown Box', a talking box with the face of a clown, filled with inviting toys. One group of children was told to withstand the temptation of Mr Clown Box by saying: 'I want to play with the fun toys later.' The achievements of this group were much better than those of the group of children which was not given an instruction by the experimenter. Other research confirms the effectiveness of such cognitive strategies. By focussing one's attention in different ways on the reward sought, resisting temptation becomes less difficult in working-situations (cf. Mischel and Underwood 1974; Patterson and Carter, 1979).

In these paradigmatic examples of self-control, children have a *preference* for obtaining the more rewarding object. They think that, all in all, the best thing to do is to accomplish the set tasks within the given time. This preference collides with certain *inclinations* however; for example, the want to respond to the tempting suggestions made by Mr Clown Box ('Look at me!', 'Play with me!'). These inclinations are then parried (whether or not one is told to do so by the experiment-leader) by applying certain forms of self-intervention, namely by directing one's concentration to the arousing properties of the reward. The frustration which results 'may serve to energize subjects' efforts toward task completion' (Patterson and Carter, 1979: 274; cf. Patterson, 1982: 294). In other words, the cognitive strategies employed result in an *increase* in the motivation to accomplish the preferred actions.

This second cluster of examples can be interpreted as cases of *stimulation*. These are instances of self-control in which the

110

actor (i) has a preference either to abstain from doing X or to perform Y; (ii) has the inclination to perform X or a counter-inclination with regard to performing Y; and (iii) intervenes with the intention of supporting his preferences with wants or aversions.

3 The virtue of self-control is a pure ability

A person exercises self-control if, and only if, he intervenes in his want(s) and/or aversion(s) with the intention of settling, in favour of his preference(s), the conflict between his preference(s) and his occurrent (counter-)inclinations – this is how the two conditions for self-control which have been described are joined together. Can we now, using this description, defend and expand the theses which were described earlier? Does the analysis which has been performed shed light on the status of the motivation theory on the one hand and on the nature of the presumed lack of self-control in present-day pupils on the other hand?

3.1 The virtue of self-control does not include specific motives

As far as the first thesis is concerned, supporters of the motivation theory claim that there is a logical connection between possessing a certain virtue and having specific motives – that is, wants and aversions with regard to certain courses of action or certain states of affairs. The virtue of fidelity, for example, includes the want to keep one's promises and an aversion with regard to breaking agreements. And the question was: can this theory also be applied to the disposition of self-control?

On the basis of our analysis of self-control we must give 'no' as an answer to this question. The description of the first condition shows *that* a preference is involved in cases of self-control. But the *content* of the preference remains undetermined. The execution of self-control does not imply a specific

111

preference. The description of the second condition reveals that the want to exercise self-control has the *same* content as the preference at stake. The agent intervenes with the intention of accomplishing *that which* he prefers. And because the content of the preference is undetermined, the same applies to the content of the want to employ self-intervention.

Attempts to link the virtue of self-control to wants and aversions with a specifiable content are thus doomed to fail. Brandt makes such an attempt when he describes a self-controlled man as 'a person who has a strong aversion to impairing his long-range prospects for a good life' (1970: 35). To put it into our terminology: in cases of self-control, a person has a preference for performances or forbearances which he considers useful for his long-term welfare. And because the want to exercise self-control has the same content as the preference, the agent interferes with the intention to accomplish *these* performances or forbearances.

The characterization of self-control as an aversion to the impairment of one's long-term welfare is too restricted however. Self-control is by no means always practised with this goal in mind. Sometimes self-intervention takes place because of a want to perform actions for their positive effects on the well-being of others. Self-control can be employed for safeguarding one's own interests as well as 'in the pursuit of the good of others' (Esheté, 1982: 508).

Until now we have assumed that the representatives of the motivation theory are defending a connection between virtues and vices on the one hand, and the *presence* of specific wants and aversions on the other. However, there is a version of the motivation theory with more nuances. According to this version, we sometimes use trait-names in order to refer to the *absence* of certain wants and aversions. According to Brandt, for example, the term '*dis*honesty' refers to a lack of honesty and thus to the '*absence* of the kind of aversion which constitutes honesty' (1970: 33). And courage is the absence of the want which is characteristic of cowardice, namely 'an all-absorbing attachment to personal safety and position' (p. 35). In the opinion of J.D. Wallace, even all the terms used for the instrumental virtues refer to the absence of motives which are characteristic of the corresponding vices (1978: 60–61). The trait-term 'temperance', for example, stands for the absence of self-indulgence, and thus for the absence of an 'excessive fondness for certain pleasures and amusements' (p. 86). Why is it out of the question that the same also applies to self-control? Perhaps this virtue is also a 'privative state'. Perhaps someone who is not in control of himself is the victim of certain (counter-)inclinations (possibly with an extraordinary causal strength). Self-control would then consist of (among other things) the *absence* of these (excessive) wants and aversions.

In my opinion, this argument does not apply either. Even if a lack of self-control always goes with extremely strong (counter-)inclinations (which I do not believe) these wants and aversions would still be undetermined as to their content. This follows from the description of the conditions necessary for exercising self-control. The results of this analysis leave completely undecided *what* (counter-)inclinations the self-controller experiences. This is also true for the statement that a person is *not* capable of controlling his wants and aversions. This assertion does not contain any implication concerning the special nature of these (counter-)inclinations either. For this reason, the disposition of self-control cannot be considered as the absence of certain (extraordinary) wants and aversions. The virtue of self-control contains neither the presence nor the absence of motives with a specifiable content.

3.2 Lack of self-control can be an expression of inability

As far as the second thesis is concerned, I have already defended the view that a possible lack of self-control in the pupils studied by Das-Smaal can be dependent on two variables. The pupil is either insufficiently motivated to control his wants and aversions or is unable to do so. If the second explanation applies, we speak of *inability*. Our analysis of self-control reveals what this inability consists of. The pupil who is afflicted with such a deficiency lacks the ability to

Jan Steutel

accomplish effective self-interventions.[10] And this ability for successful self-intervention is built up of two (clusters of) sub-abilities (cf. Patterson and Mischel, 1976: 215; Carter *et al.*, 1979: 407–408; Patterson and Carter, 1979: 274–5; Pressley, 1979: 361; Patterson, 1982: 294).

In the first place, the self-controller is capable of following *certain strategies, procedures and techniques.* The bearer of the virtue of self-control employs these means in order to change the composition and the strength of his wants and aversions in a direction which is considered favourable. Examples of such means are the techniques of self-distraction and cognitive transformation already touched on. But we can also think of less spectacular procedures such as mitigating one's impulses by counting to ten, resisting temptation by admonishing oneself, or mastering one's passions by making detailed and vivid images of the harmful long-term consequences following their gratification.[11]

In the second place, the self-controller has the ability to determine which strategies, procedures and techniques *must be applied in his own situation.* Patterson correctly suggests 'that the kinds of cognitive strategies that will be effective vary as a function of the kinds of self-control situations in which they are employed' (1982: 294). We have seen this in the above: in waiting-situations, an effective strategy is to distract one's attention from the consummatory qualities, whereas in working-situations the reverse is the case. The bearer of the virtue of self-control thus knows not only how to use strategies and techniques of self-intervention, but also knows how to identify the corresponding situations. It is quite possible that the pupils in Das-Smaal's study have acquired these sub-abilities to an insufficient degree. They thus lack the virtue of self-control.[12]

The explanation which has been presented of the virtue of self-control supports a central thought in the work of B. Spiecker (1983). In the opinion of this philosopher of education, the educational process essentially and fundamentally consists of initiating the child in rule-governed practices. Because the child is stimulated by the older generation to participate in such practices, it acquires the dispositions necessary for an adequate exercising of these practices. By *doing* the child learns to do *well*. This learning of dispositions by accomplishing the corresponding practices is called *training*.

This interpretation of the educational process fits our analysis of self-control. Exercising self-control is also a rule-governed praxis. Self-intervention consists in following *technical rules*, that is to say rules that indicate which means we must use to achieve certain ends (cf. Duintjer, 1977: 48–50). The aim of the person who controls himself is to accomplish the preferred performance or forbearance; and the means which he uses are all kinds of strategies, procedures and techniques. The bearer of the virtue of self-control is thus capable of following a great number of technical rules under the appropriate circumstances. This complex ability is acquired by training. Because the child is stimulated in the educational process to take part in many practices *in which* the practice of self-control is a must, the child learns to apply the proper strategies and techniques under the proper circumstances. Is the alleged lack of self-control in the present-day pupil attributable to an insufficient participation in such practices? Is he perhaps less trained than his predecessor?

Notes

1 The term 'disposition' is used in the same way as 'state of mind' or 'quality of mind'. In this broad sense of the word, 'disposition' applies to skills, abilities, traits of character, habits, attitudes, opinions, etc. (cf. Frankena, 1973: 20; Brezinka, 1974: 80–81).
2 Cf. Brandt (1970), Houlgate (1970) and Dent (1984). An important opponent of the motivation theory is Roberts (1984a). He questions this theory by arguing that the virtues of will power are to a large extent skill-like.
3 Brandt (1979: 166) asserts that virtues include wants and aversions not only with regard to 'behaviour of a certain sort', but also with regard to 'states of affairs'. In conformity with this conception, I formerly made a distinction between intrinsic virtues which imply wants and aversions with respect to certain *courses of action* (the non-teleological virtues), and intrinsic

virtues which include wants and aversions with respect to certain *states of affairs* (the teleological virtues) (Steutel, 1986). So, when I speak about *specific* wants and aversions, I refer to motives with regard to courses of action or states of affairs which are specifiable or determinable. In this sense of the word, not only the 'specific' virtues of R.S. Peters include specific wants and aversions, but equally his 'motivational' and 'artificial' virtues (Peters, 1981: 94–5, 104–107).

4 My criticism of the motivation theory is only valid if the disposition of self-control is in fact a virtue. It is, however, possible to question this assumption, for example by pointing out that the necessity to exercise self-control testifies rather to a *lack* of virtuousness. Aristotle (1934: 374 ff.) thus makes a distinction between two different states of character: virtue and self-control (*enkrateia*). Just like the man of virtue, the man of self-control performs the morally right actions; but unlike the former, the man of self-control has to struggle to do so because he wants to act badly (cf. Urmson, 1973).

In this context I only want to react to this objection by pointing out that (i) most supporters of the motivation theory also regard the disposition of self-control as a virtue (cf. Brandt, 1970: 35; Ryle, 1972: 444-5), and (ii) we have to make a distinction between Aristotle's man of self-control (i.e. someone who has to control his (counter-)inclinations frequently), and the bearer of the virtue of self-control (i.e. someone who is able to control his (counter-)inclinations (which has no implications with respect to the frequency of exercising this ability)).

5 This distinction between 'can' and 'want', between being capable of doing something and being motivated to do something, can be found in the publications of supporters of the so-called social learning theory. In the opinion of Mischel, it is important to make a distinction between 'the individual's *competence* [capacity] to generate... behaviors, and the motivational [incentive] variables for their *performance* in particular situations' (Mischel and Mischel, 1976: 85; cf. Mischel, 1981: 268). Mischel considers that this division between 'learning-performance' or 'competence-action' can also be applied to the phenomenon of self-control: 'On the one hand are the developmental, cognitive, and learning processes through which the abilities and skills necessary for particular novel forms of self-control are acquired in the first place. On the other hand one must consider the motivational

factors that regulate the individual's choices among the response patterns that he has already acquired' (Mischel, 1974: 252, 1976: 447; Mischel *et al.*, 1972: 217; Mischel and Mischel, 1977: 39–40).

6 It is possible to consider such cognitions as the result of a reconstructable process of practical deliberation, in which the agent weighs the (dis)advantages of various alternative actions. N.J.H. Dent (1984: 97) states that 'the emergence of a decisive preference out of deliberation is the formation by the agent of a resolution or intent to do something on the ground of its being the best thing for him to do in the circumstances'.

7 For a correct interpretation of self-control, it is important to make a distinction between *dispositional* and *occurrent* wants and aversions (cf. Steutel, 1986). If the agent exercises self-control, there has to be an occurrent want or aversion, that is to say a (counter-)inclination which is *in force*. This point is often neglected, especially by psychologists. A tippler leaves the house without money to buy liquor; a heavy smoker does not buy cigarettes for the weekend; a fat woman attaches a time-lock on her refrigerator – all these examples are simply explained as the exercise of self-control (cf. Thoresen and Mahoney, 1974). Mostly, however, such steps are taken because the person expects that his dispositional want to drink, to smoke or to eat will occur at a *later* time, and because he is afraid that he will not be able to control his occurrent inclination *at that moment*. In other words, when the agent takes action, there is no need for self-control because his dispositional want is not in force. Following D.C. Dennett (1984: 62–3), we can regard these examples as cases of *meta-level* control or *higher-order* control.

8 Various adherents of social learning theory make a distinction which is akin to my differentiation between restraint and endurance. For example, F.H. Kanfer (1971: 52, 1977: 23–31) calls these cases 'resistance to temptation' and 'tolerance of noxious stimulation' (or 'heroism') respectively; and Thoresen and Mahoney (1974: 14, 93–8) use the same words: 'restraint' (or 'decelerative self-control') and 'endurance' (or 'accelerative self-control').

9 To explain the results of the first series of experiments, Mischel and colleagues make use of an elaborated version of the so-called 'frustrative non-reward' theory (developed by A. Amsel) (cf. Mischel and Ebbesen, 1970: 335; Mischel *et al.*, 1972: 205). Not getting an expected reward elicits frustration. By focussing

attention on the reward, the aversive frustration increases. And the more intense the frustration, the more powerful the inclination to call off the experiment: 'When the distress of waiting seemed to become especially acute, children tended to reach for the termination signal' (Mischel *et al.*, 1972: 215; cf. Mischel, 1974: 267–8, 1976: 445, 1981: 249).

To interpret the results of the *second* series of experiments, the elaborated version of the frustrative non-reward theory is connected with the distinction (made by D.E. Berlyne) between the motivational (arousal) function and the cue (informative) function of stimuli. Fastening one's attention on the motivating (consummatory) qualities, increases the aversive frustration as well as the causal strength of the inclination to terminate the waiting period (cf. Mischel and Moore, 1973: 178; Mischel, 1974: 279–80; Mischel and Baker, 1975: 255, 260).

10 My interpretation of (the virtue of) self-control in terms of ability, appears to be in conformity with the view of Dennett. He proposes the following definition of 'the root idea of control' (1984: 52): 'A *controls* B if and only if the relation between A and B is such that A can *drive* B into whichever of B's normal range of states A *wants* B to be in.' In cases of self-control, he maintains, A and B are identical (cf. p. 56). In other words, a person controls himself if and only if he is *able* to drive himself into whichever of his normal range of states he wants himself to be in.

11 Fine examples of techniques to keep one's temper are set out in detail by Roberts (1984a: 246, 1984b: 400–401).

In his inspiring reflections on the problem of weakness of will in education, Straughan (1982) indicates various important techniques of self-intervention. I will give a few examples. According to Straughan, in cases of weak-willed behaviour the agent sincerely believes that he ought to do Y, while doing (or deciding to do) X. To explain this phenomenon, he discusses a great number of possible factors. He points, for example, to the fact that the agent 'fails to *concentrate* sufficiently upon the moral interpretation' or 'fails to present the moral interpretation to himself *attractively* enough' (p. 134) or 'fails to "identify" with the interests of others' (p. 214, cf. p. 143). That is why the motivation of the agent to perform Y is not strong enough. These explanations correspond with possible techniques of self-intervention: in order to control his inclination to do X, the agent can strengthen his motivation to do Y by focussing his attention on the moral aspects of his situation or by imagining an appealing moral interpretation of his situation or by trying to identify with the interests of others.

12 What is the relation between lacking the virtue of self-control and weakness of will? Straughan seems to reject all explanations and definitions of weakness of will in terms of lack of self-control. According to him, cases of weakness of will must satisfy the ability criterion: the weak-willed agent is physically and psychologically capable of acting (and choosing) otherwise (cf. 1982: 82-5); and someone who is out of control is missing this ability (cf. pp. 71, 93). I think, however, that the classes of weakness of will and lack of self-control partly coincide. Several illustrations of weakness of will in Straughan's book, for example the weak-willed smoker (pp. 137-8), or drinking, drugtaking and sexual promiscuity (p. 157), can also quite naturally be regarded as deficiencies in the ability to control oneself.

References

Alston, W.P. (1977). Self-intervention and the Structure of Motivation. *In* Th. Mischel (ed.), *The Self. Psychological and Philosophical Issues*, pp. 65–102. Oxford.

Aristotle (1934). *Nicomachean Ethics*. Edited by G.P. Goold. Cambridge, Mass.

Brandt, R.B. (1970). Traits of Character: A Conceptual Analysis. *American Philosophical Quarterly*, 7, 23–37.

Brandt, R.B. (1979). *A Theory of the Good and the Right*. Oxford.

Brezinka, W. (1974). *Grundbegriffe der Erziehungswissenschaft. Analyse, Kritik, Vorschläge*. München/Basel.

Carter, D.B., Patterson, C.J. and Quasebarth, S.J. (1979). Development of Children's Use of Plans for Self-control. *Cognitive Therapy and Research*, 3, 407–13.

Das-Smaal, E. (1985). Huidige leerling is ongeduriger en sneller afgeleid. *Didaktief*, 15, 16–18.

Das-Smaal, E.A., Leeuw, L. de and Orlebeke, J.F. (1987). Is er iets mis met de aandacht van het schoolkind? *Pedagogische Studiën*, 64, 1–15.

Dennett, D.C. (1984). *Elbow Room. The Varieties of Free Will Worth Wanting*. Oxford.

Dent, N.J.H. (1984). *The Moral Psychology of the Virtues*.

Cambridge.

Duintjer, O.D. (1977). *Rondom regels. Wijsgerige gedachten omtrent regel-geleid gedrag*. Meppel/Amsterdam.

Esheté, A. (1982). Character, Virtue and Freedom. *Philosophy*, **57**, 495–513.

Foot, Ph. (1978). *Virtues and Vices and Other Essays in Moral Philosophy*. Berkeley and Los Angeles.

Frankena, W.K. (1973). The Concept of Education Today. *In* J.F. Doyle (ed.), *Educational Judgments. Papers in the Philosophy of Education*, pp. 19–32. London and Boston.

Houlgate, L.D. (1970). Virtue is Knowledge. *The Monist*, 142–53.

Kanfer, F.H. (1971). The Maintenance of Behavior by Self-generated Stimuli and Reinforcement. *In* A. Jacobs and L.B. Sachs (eds), *The Psychology of Private Events. Perspectives on Covert Response Systems*, pp. 39–59. New York and London.

Kanfer, F.H. (1977). The Many Faces of Self-control, or Behavior Modification Changes its Focus. *In* R.B. Stuart (ed.), *Behavioral Self-management: Strategies, Techniques and Outcomes*, pp. 1–48. New York.

Mackie, J.L. (1980). *Hume's Moral Theory*. London.

Mischel, W. (1974). Processes in Delay of Gratification. *In* L. Berkowitz (ed.), *Advances in Experimental Social Psychology*, pp. 249–92. New York.

Mischel, W. (1976). *Introduction to Personality*. New York.

Mischel, W. (1981). Metacognition and the Rules of Delay. *In* J.H. Flavell and L. Ross (eds), *Social Cognitive Development. Frontiers and Possible Futures*, pp. 240–71. Cambridge.

Mischel, W. and Baker, N. (1975). Cognitive Appraisals and Transformations in Delay Behavior. *Journal of Personality and Social Psychology*, **31**, 245–61.

Mischel, W. and Ebbesen, E.B. (1970). Attention in Delay of Gratification. *Journal of Personality and Social Psychology*, **16**, 329–37.

Mischel, W. and Mischel, H.N. (1976). A Cognitive Social-learning Approach to Morality and Self-regulation. *In* Th. Lickona (ed.), *Moral Development and Moral Behavior. Theory, Research, and Social Issues*, pp. 84–107. New York.

Mischel, W. and Mischel, H.N. (1977). Self-control and the Self. *In* Th. Mischel (ed.), *The Self. Psychological and Philosophical Issues*, pp. 31–64. Oxford.

Mischel, W. and Moore, B. (1973). Effects of Attention to

Symbolically Presented Rewards on Self-control. *Journal of Personality and Social Psychology*, **28**, 172–9.

Mischel, W. and Moore, B. (1980). The Role of Ideation in Voluntary Delay of Symbolically Presented Rewards. *Cognitive Therapy and Research*, **4**, 211–21.

Mischel, W. and Patterson, C.J. (1976). Substantive and Structural Elements of Effective Plans for Self-control. *Journal of Personality and Social Psychology*, **34**, 942–50.

Mischel, W. and Underwood, B. (1974). Instrumental Ideation in Delay of Gratification. *Child Development*, **45**, 1083–88.

Mischel, W., Ebbesen, E.B. and Zeiss, A. (1972). Cognitive and Attentional Mechanisms in Delay of Gratification. *Journal of Personality and Social Psychology*, **21**, 204–18.

Moore, B.S. (1977). Cognitive Representation of Rewards in Delay of Gratification. *Cognitive Therapy and Research*, **1**, 73–83.

Moore, B., Mischel, W. and Zeiss, A. (1976). Comparative Effects of the Reward Stimulus and its Cognitive Representation in Voluntary Delay. *Journal of Personality and Social Psychology*, **34**, 419–24.

Patterson, C.J. (1982). Self-control and Self-regulation in Childhood. *In* T.M. Field *et al.* (eds), *Review of Human Development*, pp. 290–303. New York.

Patterson, C.J. and Carter, D.B. (1979). Attentional Determinants of Children's Self-control in Waiting and Working Situations. *Child Development*, **50**, 272–5.

Patterson, C.J. and Mischel, W. (1976). Effects of Temptation-inhibiting and Task-facilitating Plans on Self-control. *Journal of Personality and Social Psychology*, **33**, 209–17.

Peters, R.S. (1981). *Moral Development and Moral Education*. London.

Pressley, M. (1979). Increasing Children's Self-control through Cognitive Interventions. *Review of Educational Research*, **49**, 319–70.

Roberts, R.C. (1984a). Will Power and the Virtues. *The Philosophical Review*, **93**, 227–47.

Roberts, R.C. (1984b). Solomon on the Control of Emotions. *Philosophy and Phenomenological Research*, **44**, 395–412.

Ryle, G. (1958). On Forgetting the Difference between Right and Wrong. *In* A.I. Melden (ed.), *Essays in Moral Philosophy*, pp. 147–59. Seattle and London.

Ryle, G. (1972). Can Virtue be Taught? *In* R.F. Dearden, P.H. Hirst and R.S. Peters (eds), *Education and the Development of Reason*, pp. 434–47. London and Boston.

Spiecker, B. (1983). 'Kunnen' en 'Kennen' in de vroeg-kinderlijke ontwikkeling. Een theoretisch-pedagogische verhandeling. *Pedagogische Studiën*, 60, 165–72.

Steutel, J.W. (1986). Education, Motives and Virtues. *Journal of Moral Education*, 15, 179–88.

Straughan, R. (1982). *'I Ought to, but...' A Philosophical Approach to the Problem of Weakness of Will in Education*. Windsor.

Thoresen, C.E. and Mahoney, M.J. (1974). *Behavioral Self-control*. New York.

Urmson, J.O. (1973). Aristotle's Doctrine of the Mean. *American Philosophical Quarterly*, 10, 223–30.

Wallace, J.D. (1978). *Virtues and Vices*. Ithaca and London.

Index

Index

Index

shame, 46–7
Shotter, J., 52
Sidgwick, H., 64
Simon, S., 15
Skinner, B.F., 9, 92
Slote, M., 1, 3, 40n
Snik, G., 40n
social-learning theory, 116–17n
Socrates, 93
Spiecker, B., 1–2, 114
stages, 25–37, 38–40n; of
    conceptualization, 24, 27–31; of
    moderation, 72–3; of moral
    judgement, 18–23, 35–6, 56;
    qualitative differences between,
    26–8
Steutel, J.W., 1, 4–5, 46, 50, 116–17n
Straughan, R.R., 1–2, 4, 10, 12–13,
    118–19n
subjectivism, 83, 87

Thoresen, C.E., 117n
Thorndike, E., 92–4
Thornton, D., 34
Thornton, S., 34
training, 5, 8–9, 80, 115; and
    practice, 77, 79
Turiel, E., 88, 91

Underwood, B., 110
Urmson, J.O., 116n

virtue(s), 3–5, 92–4, 100–1, 111–13;
    artificial, 46, 53, 56, 60n; and
    competence, 77, 91–6; and

development, 37, 40n; and
    emotions, 44–7, 50, 53;
    instrumental, 66, 102–3, 113;
    intrinsic, 115n; of moderation, 3,
    64–73; motivation theory of, 5,
    100–1, 103–4, 111–13, 115–16n;
    natural, 47, 54, 56, 60n; (non-)
    teleological, 46–7, 115–16n; of
    prudence, 82, 93; of self-control,
    4–5, 99–119
Vuyk, R., 24

Wallace, J.D., 112
wants/aversions, 4–5, 100–1, 105,
    111–13, 115–16n; as (counter)
    inclinations, 4, 11–13, 102–6,
    109–10, 113, 116n; as preferences,
    104–6, 109–10, 117n; and self-
    control, 100–4, 111–13
Warnock, G.J., 55, 59n
weakness (moral-), 4–5, 9–13,
    118–19n; and education, 13–16;
    and judgement, 10; and reasons,
    11–13; and self-control, 119n; and
    self-deception, 13–14
White, J., 44, 47
will power, 10, 115n
Williams, B., 43, 55
Williams, H., 16
Willmann, O., 81, 85
Wilson, J., 59n
Wispé, L., 47

Zajonc, R.B., 48, 60n

126